GW00384217

Where We Used to Work

Where We Used to Work

Kenneth Hudson

John Baker
London

First published 1980
John Baker (Publishers) Ltd
35 Bedford Row, London WC1R 4JH

© Kenneth Hudson 1980

ISBN 0 212 97025 9

Hudson, Kenneth
    Where we used to work.
    1. Labor and laboring classes – Great Britain
    – History
    I. Title
    331.7.00942   HD8390

    ISBN 0–212–97025–9

Text set in 11/12 pt VIP Bembo, printed and bound
in Great Britain at The Pitman Press, Bath

Contents

List of illustrations

Introduction

Over the years, a great deal has been written about the Egyptian pyramids. Generation after generation of archaeologists and historians have given their views on how these prodigious monuments were built, how the materials were brought to the site, how the labour force was recruited and organised, how the projects were financed and, most important of all, what significance such great piles of stones had for the Egyptians themselves. Theories have been announced, challenged, discarded, replaced; reputations have been made or lost; assumptions and deductions have been confidently presented as if they were facts. The pyramids are still there, and every year thousands of more or less well-informed tourists make what they choose of them.

One thing is certain. If, by some miracle, we were able to talk to a few of the people who actually built the pyramids – the architects, masons, labourers, court go-betweeners – we should be compelled to remodel history in a fairly thoroughgoing way. Many of the theories propounded with such conviction by British experts, German experts, French experts and all the rest of the highly respected scholarly tribe would undoubtedly prove to be at best in need of considerable revision and at worst utter nonsense. Yesterday's Egyptian common man, rescued from his anonymity, would become a serious embarrassment to today's historians.

And not only the Egyptian common man, of course. Interviews with simple Romans, rank-and-file Vikings, early Christians, Elizabethan sailors and members of Napoleon's armies would assuredly upset the historical apple-cart in a most disturbing fashion. For the peace of mind of most professional historians, it is better that such ghosts should not be permitted to arise from their graves. But history does not exist primarily for historians, any more than politics exists for politicians and health and disease for doctors. What matters – the only thing that matters – is that we should be moving all the time towards a more accurate, more balanced understanding of the past. And

1

in the creation of that understanding the common man – the Roman bricklayer, the eighteenth century foundry-worker, the Victorian carpenter, coal-miner and engine-driver – has a vital part to play. The history which is written solely or mainly from the information supplied by owners and managers is as false, one-sided and misleading as the history which comes only from the shop floor. Nothing but the full range of fact and opinion will do, and how seldom is that full range available.

But information is not derived, of course, only from reminiscences. With industrial history, as with all other varieties of history, every shred of evidence about the past is relevant. One extra and apparently insignificant clue can make sense of the mass of half-understood knowledge one already has.

I have been writing books about industrial history and industrial archaeology for twenty years and during the past seven or eight of these years it has gradually impressed itself on me that the traditional academic sharing out of the past into subjects called economic history, architectural history, social history, the history of technology, industrial archaeology and so on may be professionally convenient and profitable but makes little real sense. One kind of historical evidence is so dependent on all the others that to think of our ancestors only in terms of wages, prices, tools, housing, health, profits, machinery, or whatever one's own particular scholarly speciality happens to be is to condemn oneself to toiling in blinkers. Specialisation would not matter so much if the different breeds of specialists were regularly in close contact with one another, exchanging and pooling their discoveries in a fruitful and friendly manner. But, with very rare exceptions, they are not. They read their own specialised periodicals, attend their own specialised conferences, write their own specialised books. There is not a great deal of cross-fertilisation of ideas between the members of one academic department and another, and scholarship is the poorer for it.

It is an unsatisfactory situation, brought about by the sheer accumulation of facts and theories which has burdened the world increasingly during the past 150 years or so: with so much to know and to sift, how can a man be expected to do more than cultivate one tiny patch? If he refuses to do this, finding extreme specialisation mentally crippling and inhuman, and makes an attempt to bring different lines of enquiry, wider fields of evidence, together in his mind, it is very likely that he will find the academic world's sharpest arrow aimed at him. He will be branded a generalist.

The Victorians were luckier and wiser in this respect. The point is well made in an obituary of the historian, barrister and Member of Parliament, Sir Henry Howarth, who was born in 1842 and lived on happily until 1923.

'It is the fashion now to make the age an age of specialists, but Sir Henry Howarth did not conform to that fashion. He was rather of those who, like Bacon, take all knowledge for their province, and so he was often able to suggest analogies between one subject and another which would not occur to the specialist, and it may be that much of the usefulness of his contributions to knowledge is to be traced to this fact. That he had so many interests may also explain the extraordinary freshness of his mind to the end of his eighty-one years.'

It may well be so – Victorian scholars certainly had the habit of reaching their eightieth birthday in remarkably good condition – but Howarth's instinct for crossing academic frontiers is distinctly unpopular nowadays. This is a curious state of affairs, since there is no more demanding and rewarding task than to take a great mass of historical bits and pieces and find a pattern and a meaning in them. The past is not a neat and tidy affair – that is its fascination – and the historian's business is to try to impose a shape and order on the ragbag of facts which constitutes his raw material. The bigger his ragbag, the wider he ranges in search of his evidence, the more difficult his job is bound to be and the greater the satisfaction when he reaches the end of it. It is probably true that the successful generalist needs to have a different temperament from the successful specialist, and probably a tougher hide, but that is no reason to regard his efforts and techniques as inferior.

It is important to make this point as strongly as possible, because industrial archaeology is just beginning to find its way out of a maze which is entirely of its own making. Industrial archaeology is a type of study which can, properly handled, provide useful additional information about the way in which previous generations of people earned a living and, in the process, served the community. By concentrating on the physical remains of yesterday's factories, warehouses, machinery, shops, housing and transport systems, it is possible to learn a great deal about the organisation, scale and environment of work fifty, a hundred, two hundred years ago. The archaeology, in other words, can supplement and frequently modify what is already known from the written and printed records and it can set in motion completely new lines of enquiry.

One has, alas, to say 'can supplement', rather than 'supplements', because a great deal of the work carried out by industrial archaeologists has been largely or completely sterile, comparable to the singleminded collection of postage stamps, coins or matchbox labels. Any archaeological work, industrial or otherwise, has a point only if it is carried out with the kind of informed imaginative understanding which allows the archaeologist to think and feel his way back into the lives of the people who created what he is studying. To go on, year after year, discovering and recording old watermills, steam engines, tram depots, potteries or whatever the chosen sites may be is pointless and, for most people, eventually unsatisfying unless one is constantly asking oneself the question, 'What did this mean at the time when it was working?' And this question can be sensibly put and answered only by cultivating a willingness to think locally, on the small scale, rather more than nationally, on the big scale.

The difficulty has been that industrial archaeologists, at all levels, have allowed their enthusiasm to run away with them. They have made absurdly exaggerated claims for what they regard as their 'subject'. Industrial archaeology, however, is not really a 'subject' at all, but rather a very useful emphasis on certain categories of historical material, material which had, until the industrial archaeology movement got under way in the 1960s, been unreasonably neglected. For a number of years, until the mid-Seventies, industrial archaeologists considered the main problem facing them to be one of preservation – how could this or that mill, power station, coal-mine or tram depot be saved from demolition? Since then, an increasingly numerous band of heretics has been pointing out that mere preservation is not enough and that what really matters is interpretation, deciding what significance a particular industrial monument had within the life of the community where it was situated and, in a very few instances, within the general industrial, technological or social history of the nation.

This book, *Where We Used to Work*, is concerned with real people in real places – a particular construction site, a particular furniture workshop, a particular aircraft factory – not with abstractions about the construction industry, the furniture industry, the aircraft industry. Nobody works in retailing. They work for a branch of Marks and Spencer or Debenhams or for the sweet and paper shop in Fore Street, each of which has its own atmosphere, its own customers, its own staff relationships and its own special good and bad points. And the same is true of bus-driving, cake-making, car-assembly, tax-collecting, hairdressing or any other kind of job one cares to name. One can speak with assurance only about the local unit, the individual workplace. Anything bigger than that is a half-truth, a second best, an entity to be approached with the greatest caution.

The industries selected for discussion and illustration cover a wide spectrum, from gloving to aeroplanes and from sorting and delivering letters to printing. The method has been the same in each case. First, there is a brief account of the firm and its history, drawn up from various printed sources. Then there are one or two photographs to show what the workplace looked like at some relevant point in the recent past, usually

4

between twenty and fifty years ago. And finally there are the memories of one or two people who worked there.

The whole item represents an attempt to illustrate the value of combining different kinds of evidence and to provide examples of the type of information which is extremely unlikely to find its way into print in the ordinary way. The people involved have been allowed to tell the story in their own way. What they said in front of the microphone has not been changed or 'improved', although parts have been removed, to avoid unnecessary repetitions and remove material which does not relate directly to the theme. After the tape had been transcribed, each person was sent a copy of the typescript and asked to do three things: check for simple inaccuracies, such as a wrong date or name, indicate anything which the informant would prefer, for one reason or another, not to have published, and add facts which did not come to mind at the time the interview was carried out, but which, on reflection, seem interesting or important. The result is what can be read here – work as a particular man or woman remembers it.

These personal accounts often contain facts and comments which come as a surprise to the public relations department and managers of the firms in question. From an official point of view, such revelations are not always entirely welcome, but there has never been any attempt to censor them. On the contrary, there have been many occasions when transcripts of ex-employees' reminiscences have produced additional information, including old photographs, from the company itself. That is one of the great advantages of this kind of research. There is a snowball effect, with a chance sentence unearthing a mass of previously unsuspected material.

Clearly, the more the interviewer knows to begin with, the more he is likely to get from the people he talks to. It is foolish to switch on the tape recorder without having previously visited the place that is to be discussed and, so far as one can, familiarised oneself with its history. One should arrive with a pretty good knowledge of the building, the processes and the products, together with a general idea of the changes which have taken place in recent years. Without this, it is difficult, if not impossible, to ask the most fruitful questions. The purpose of the interview is twofold – to fill gaps in one's knowledge and to obtain more reliable bearings, by finding out how the job seemed to a person who actually performed it day after day.

Talking around a photograph or a site-plan is often very helpful. One can then make one's questions more precise, by asking, for example, 'What's the man in the corner of the picture doing?', or 'Wasn't it difficult to work with those machines so close together?' or 'Can you remember the names of the people we're looking at in the photograph?' Sometimes it is useful to tour the buildings with someone who once worked in them, asking him to remember how things were in his working days. In my experience, people respond remarkably well to this kind of practical, immediate stimulus. What they are doing, in effect, is to bring the archaeology alive, to give it a human dimension. One can organise this quite easily for the industrial archaeology of the past fifty years or so; students of earlier periods are obviously at a disadvantage. How wonderful, and no doubt how humbling, it would be to be able to talk to the veterans who dug the eighteenth century canals, built the early Victorian railways or tapped Abraham Darby's first coke-fired iron furnace. How grateful historians would be now for records of interviews carried out at the time.

Even so, everything has to have a beginning and the fact that, so far as we know, nobody interviewed the first generation of engine-drivers or the power-loom operators is no reason for shirking the duty of collecting the memories of nylon-spinners, car assembly workers or air hostesses. Workers are, in fact, a vital part of the archaeology of industry. So long as they are obliging enough to remain alive, they are as much archaeological material as a building or a machine is, a fact which the Japanese have sensibly acknowledged by designating certain veterans as industrial or handicraft monuments, to be revered and suitably pensioned and used as sources of information and inspiration. The attempt to keep objects in one compartment and the people who used those objects in another is misguided and stultifying. Both have to be held in the same focus and studied together, if the historical record is to stand any chance at all of completeness and fairness.

What seems to be needed is a new title for what has been known for the past twenty years as industrial archaeology. Work archaeology might do very well. It has a dynamic, human flavour about it, and bypasses the sterile obsession with inanimate survivals with which industrial archaeology has become identified. It avoids, too, tedious arguments as to what is and what is not 'industrial'. 'Work archaeology' is a much more flexible name. It relates to the physical remains, human and non-human, of yesterday's ways of making a living by making, distributing, moving and selling things, and consequently includes the worlds of shops, banks and laboratories as happily and easily as railway stations and gasworks.

This book is an invitation to regard industrial history as part of social history, a pioneering essay on the techniques and merits of work archaeology, a term which now appears for the first time in print. For the record, its original public appearance was at a lecture I gave at the South Australian Museum, Adelaide, on 24th May 1979.

The examples chosen for study here are essentially illustrative. They are presented in the hope and belief that they will encourage many other people to carry out similar research in their own areas and with quite different industries and occupations. There is a great urgency about such investigations. 1930, we need to keep reminding ourselves, is half a century ago and anyone beginning work then is now in his or her mid-sixties, with not much time left for reminiscence. If the memories of these veterans are to be collected at all, they have to be collected now.

It is not, of course, suggested that other postmen, printers, furniture-makers, chefs and waitresses might not produce evidence which would contradict some of the information provided in the following pages. One person's experiences are never quite the same as another's and certain aspects of the past undergo a transformation with the passage of years. If the intention were to produce a comprehensive history of restaurants or of the postal service in the Twenties and Thirties, one would necessarily proceed quite differently, although the element of personal reminiscence is always needed, in order to give reality and balance to the official record. The fact is, and it cannot be over-emphasised, that unless the experiences of members of the ordinary work-force of any industry, trade or profession and the photographs and personal documents to illustrate those experiences are somehow discovered, written down and preserved, the historians of the near and the distant future will be deprived of essential working material. Their evidence will be distorted and their judgement impaired. Gathering information of this kind is a task which can be carried out adequately only with the help of a considerable number of people, working in the areas which are familiar to them. This book is an attempt to show not only how this can be done and what the results are but, more important, how such reminiscences form a natural and indispensable part of a local historical context. Without an awareness of the context – the place, the industry, the time, the politics, current concepts of discipline and justice, the spirit of the age – much of the value of interviews and conversations is likely to be lost. Work archaeology has many ingredients and this book tries to indicate what they are and how they inter-relate.

Some readers may wonder why the material relating to the construction of Clifton Cathedral has been put first in the arrangement of the chapters. The main reason for this is a wish to begin on a note of optimism, with a recent industrial project on which everyone directly concerned was contented, a contemporary moral tale. One could very easily have chosen a construction site with the most depressing associations – strikes and delays, poor management, disgruntled workers, deplorable workmanship – a place of which nobody was proud. The

Barbican, in the City of London, would have been an excellent example, and there would have been no difficulty in finding and persuading people who worked on this ill-fated scheme to pour out their experiences into a tape-recorder and in taking photographs to show what happens when nobody cares how the job is done. This is the all too familiar and much publicised side of the construction industry. One cannot deny the Barbicans; they exist in plenty up and down the country. But the first-class buildings tend to be pushed into the background, so that what is revealed by talking to the men who worked on Clifton Cathedral is likely to come as a great surprise to many people. If one had not located the men, talked to them and matched their comments with the pictures, the building of the cathedral would have been documented in a very incomplete way, and the real feelings of skilled workers about the state of the construction industry and about what was needed to put matters right and to give men a pride in their work would have been not so much suppressed as allowed to go by default.

For these reasons, the book deliberately begins with a plus, and it does not seem necessary to apologise for that.

Finding the pictures

It is, alas, an illusion that the history of our own times is easier to research and write than the history of a century or more ago. There are the most extraordinary gaps in information. Consider, for instance, what is and is not available in the case of newspapers. There is, in most cases, no great problem about files of the newspapers themselves. One can consult them either at the offices of the newspaper, or at a public library or in the British Library's Newspaper Library at Colindale, North London. Sometimes, it is true, the facilities available for the student are very cramped and sometimes squalid. Frequently nowadays one has to make do, not with original copies, but with that wretchedly inconvenient and time-wasting makeshift, the microfilm and microfilm projector. But, in one way or another, the papers are there. The premises and staff, however, are quite another matter. Newspapers live by pictures and they are continuously taking and receiving photographs to illustrate their stories. These photographs, more or less efficiently filed and indexed, are available to the public. One can, given time and patience, look at them and buy prints. What one cannot do, however, except in very rare instances, is discover photographs dealing with the newspaper's own activities. Nobody, it appears, has ever thought to take a picture of the editor's office, the wire room, the machine room, the newsroom or the reporters' room, as they were in 1920, 1930 or any other date one cares to mention. Visually, the centre of the spider's web of the *Guardian*, the *Bristol Evening Post*, the *Southampton Echo* or the *Yorkshire Post* is, for all practical purposes, undocumented.

Much the same is true of shops and department stores. Large concerns, such as Tesco, Whiteley's, Maples or Selfridges, have the most pitiful historical archives, especially where pictures are concerned. For the Twenties and Thirties, it is most uncommon for them to possess anything much better than the occasional exterior or catalogue. Pictures taken inside the sales area or workrooms are virtually non-existent. If they were ever commissioned, they have long since disappeared, much to the annoyance, it should be said, of the archives, publicity and public relations departments of the companies themselves, nowadays constantly under pressure to produce books, brochures or exhibitions about the history of the firm.

The main reason for this unfortunate lack of visual documentation is a perfectly understandable concentration, year after year, on making a profit and keeping the business going. That is still the situation, and it is by no means certain that future historians will be any better provided with pictures relating to 1980 than present historians with pictures of 1950 or 1930, although one hopes they will be. Even among enlightened concerns, however, someone has to give an answer to the extremely difficult question, 'What do we keep?' Each month produces another crop of paper and it is obviously impossible and ridiculous to keep all of it. But the imagination required to sense which items are likely to be of most interest or significance to posterity is a rare gift, and, faced with such a daunting task, even the best of archivists can only do his best. According to temperament, he can be comforted or depressed by knowing that he is bound to make mistakes.

Sometimes, of course, the decision-making is looked after by Fate. The Second World War thinned out company records in a very ruthless and undiscriminating fashion. Great quantities of records were sacrificed to the national hunger for waste paper and tons more were the innocent victims of German bombing raids. Of the firms mentioned in the present book, Illustrated Newspapers – an unusually archive-conscious concern – lost a high proportion of its precious and carefully conserved pre-1939 material, including many hundreds of original nineteenth century drawings, and the great gloving firm, Dents, said goodbye to practically every record it possessed, in the course of an air-raid on the City of London.

For these various reasons, discovering the pictures one wants and needs is a difficult and frustrating business, although it certainly has its moments of excitement and triumph. Many of the illustrations in the following pages have come from what one might call official sources – company archives and public collections of one kind and another – but many more, including a high proportion of the most interesting, have simply emerged as souvenirs and mementoes from the homes of pensioners. Finding them has been one of the major pleasures of preparing this book.

These photographs and documents have become family possessions in a variety of ways, some legal, some not. When the old servant of a company clears out his desk and shelves before disappearing into retirement, he may well find it extremely difficult to remember and decide which items are strictly his and which belong to his employer. The line between the two is often hard to draw. Anyone who has worked for half a century for the same firm is fully entitled to think of himself as part of the history of the place and to regard old photographs, programmes and brochures as barnacles which have gathered around him over the years. But, apart from this kind of material, there is frequently documentation of a more personal and social nature – group photographs, pictures of presentations, certificates, press cuttings, letters – and this can be a very rewarding and agreeable source of information, woven inextricably into the lives and memories of the people concerned. They are a vital part of what we have called work archaeology, clues to the experience of earning a living.

If one has to name one group or category of person as being of outstanding importance in the conservation of this very important historical material, there is no doubt that it has to be widows. These are the people into whose hands the great mass of modest, personal industrial relics passes after the death of the men who accumulated it. They have the ultimate power, in most cases, to burn or to help. The wish to tidy up is always in competition with an instinct to hold on to the past, and it is often nothing more than a whim or a passing mood that decides the issue.

The company archivist and the industrial historian both need widows very badly. Contacting widows is, in fact, a prime historical skill, to be ranked with the art of getting on good terms with the pensioners themselves. It is worth mentioning, perhaps, that those companies which attach great importance to keeping in touch with their old employees and with their families – the English China Clays Group does this in model fashion, through its house magazine and in other ways – also tend to have the richest and most comprehensive photographic archives.

Sometimes one has to accept and use photographs of very indifferent quality, simply because nothing else exists. This is not necessarily a disadvantage. There is something very moving about, for instance, a faded, creased picture of six little Post Office messenger boys, taken sixty years ago. For all its technical imperfections it makes a far greater impact than a sharp, clear professional photograph in mint condition would. This represents the beginning of a man's long career with the Post Office, a memento preserved all his life, transferred repeatedly from pocket to drawer to envelope to desk and frequently taken out and shown to friends and relations. It is a used, well-worn photograph and it is this, as much as the subject matter, that is the source of its charm. Thought of in conjunction with the very detailed memories of one of the boys looking at the camera so long ago, it has a powerful ability to recall the past, not only intellectually but emotionally.

Few old photographs convey only facts. They give us a sense of mood, of atmosphere, and sometimes this can be recaptured in a very general way. One eating-house, one furniture-workshop, one aeroplane assembly-shop of fifty years ago can speak for many others. 'This,' it says in effect, 'is how things were at the time when I was a waitress/cabinet-maker/aircraft fitter in my twenties.' Where no picture of exactly the right workplace exists, it is often better to include something of the same period than to leave a person's reminiscences to speak for themselves, especially since the publication of one photograph not infrequently causes others to appear from previously unsuspected sources. A large part of the nation's history is still hiding away in funny places and one reason for writing and publishing a book is, paradoxically, to discover material of all kinds which one would have been extremely grateful to have been aware of when one was carrying out the research for the book. This is known as the unlocking factor and it is one of the chief reasons for writing books.

Chapter One   'An ecclesiastical bargain'

The Church of SS Peter and Paul, the new cathedral for the Roman Catholic diocese of Clifton, was consecrated on 29th June 1973. It was one of the first in the world to meet the requirements of the new forms of worship laid down for Catholics by the Second Vatican Council in 1965, which emphasise the active role which everyone in the congregation plays in worship. Clifton Cathedral was designed to allow each person present to see and hear clearly what the priest is doing at the altar and to feel part of whatever is taking place. The congregation is grouped fan-wise around the high altar in such a way that nobody is more than fifty feet from it. The altar is in open view. There is nothing resembling the traditional nave, with its forest of pillars.

The brief given to the architects, the Percy Thomas Partnership, was to produce a building of high quality – the Bishop stipulated a minimum life of three hundred years – with low maintenance costs, at a price which was not to exceed £500,000, exclusive of professional fees and the cost of the site. The construction contract was given to John Laing and Son, Ltd, and the work was completed in a little over three years. Laing's, with justifiable pride, described it as 'the fastest cathedral project undertaken in Britain' – the new Coventry Cathedral, another Laing project, took seven years – and the Diocese, having studied the building costs of other comparable buildings, believed it had 'an ecclesiastical bargain of the Seventies'.

The architectural design is ingenious. Basically the structure consists of three ascending rings of concrete walls, increasing in depth towards the sanctuary. The ring enclosing the nave, sanctuary, weekday chapel and font becomes a deep beam supported on columns and walls ten feet above the main floor level. The star beam over the sanctuary and nave is the most important structural element in the building. It spans a space 106 ft. by 125 ft. at its widest point and supports the roof over the nave and the cupola over the sanctuary.

Clifton Cathedral. View from Pembroke Road, looking towards the Portal of St Peter.

Two of the star beam's arms extend and project upwards into the hexagonal space above the sanctuary and through the split-level cupola roof to form the two 68 ft. high front arms of the reinforced concrete fleche. The space above the sanctuary is surmounted by the cupola, from which the three-pronged fleche rises into the sky. The thrust from the cupola and the fleche is resisted by a ring beam, which sits above the star beam.

The hexagonal basic plan uses an equilateral triangle with a height of 1 ft. 6 in. as the module controlling all dimensions and angles of the building. This means that the structure contains practically no right angles and, since the material chosen was in situ reinforced concrete, extreme accuracy of workmanship was essential. Most of the sources of light are at roof level and are arranged so that the intensity of light increases from the perimeter of the building to the high altar.

The acoustic treatment is remarkable. In most churches, the acoustics are a compromise, being either too reverberant for speech or too dead for organ music, but at Clifton the structure allows the nave and the sanctuary to be separately tuned, so that the nave has the correct reverberation time for speech, while the roof and walls of the sanctuary, into which the organ sound is projected, can be kept at a longer reverberation time, to improve the quality of the organ music.

The environmental consultants decided that the cheapest form of heating the building would be to use an electric under-floor system and to treat the whole building as a thermal storage unit. This demanded a thick concrete envelope, capable of storing the heat, together with excellent insulation on the outside of the envelope. The walls are covered with two inches of expanded polystyrene and the cladding panels are fixed on top of that. The roof consists of six inches of concrete, covered first with expanded polystyrene, then with felt and finally with lead.

A very high level of workmanship was essential. The erection

Clifton Cathedral. The nave, looking over the sanctuary towards the baptistry and gallery. This picture shows the complex nature of the concrete structure, with practically no right angles, and indicates the great care that had to be taken with the shuttering and the quality of the concrete.

15

of the cathedral was an exceptionally difficult process, due partly to the unusual design and partly to the need to achieve a good quality finish in in situ concrete. The work-force was hand-picked, very little use was made of sub-contractors and the whole task was planned and carried through by a site agent, Bill Barnes, of quite outstanding ability. Mr Barnes unfortunately died before the project was completed.

Because of the shape of the building and the work sequence adopted, no tower crane was used. A hoist dealt with the in situ concrete material and a mobile crane was employed for fixing the pre-cast cladding panels. All the shuttering was manhandled into position and its super-accurate construction was a matter of cabinet-making rather than carpentry.

This was, in fact, the kind of contract that the great majority of today's building workers never have the chance to work on, a job on which there was no cutting of corners and where only the best workmanship was tolerated. The cathedral is there for anyone to look at, and three hundred years from now our descendants will be able to judge it as a monument of building technology. The plans and specifications and the contractor's records will be available for study in some archive or library, unless fire, flood or war has obliterated them, and the files of the architectural journals will be there to tell the historian what the various professionals thought about the building at the time of its opening. What is almost certain to be missing is the kind of information we should value so much in the case of the medieval cathedrals – the reminiscences and opinions of the men who actually carried out the work, and whose experiences do so much to enrich, humanise, and not infrequently correct the official record of what took place.

Two of the team of men who built Clifton Cathedral were Jock Ruttledge, the foreman joiner, and Alan Mansfield, the general foreman. They were on the site from beginning to end and they both agreed that it was the job of a lifetime. This is how it remained fixed in the memory of Alan Mansfield:

'It was a one-off job. I've been in the building trade all my life, too many years to remember now, 33 or 34 years, and it's the first job I've been on like that, where we've had a module system for measuring. Everything was built to a module. All the designs and everything worked on that module system. Very interesting, we found. My friend, Len Wilshire, who was the Engineer, found it quite exciting at times, which doesn't happen very much on a building site.

'The module was new for us to work to. I'd never worked before on a building that was six-sided, with no 90° angles anywhere. Everything was worked on a six-sided figure.'

The standards required for the concrete amazed him, too.

'In the trade we used to nickname it "rice pudding". It was

beautiful, just like rice pudding. We had to have that mix to obtain the wood grain on the concrete.'

The coarse aggregate was limestone from a quarry near Frome and the fine aggregate a light-coloured sand from Wareham, in Dorset. It was a special mix, 45% $\frac{3}{4}-\frac{1}{2}$ in. limestone, 25% $\frac{1}{4}$ in. limestone and 30% white sand, with a cement to aggregate ratio of 1 to 4.8.

'The strength was quite high, probably twice as much as we usually work on. The strength of concrete we normally use would be about 3,000 lbs per square inch and here it was about 6,000, so it was quite high.

'After we had what we call a strike – that means taking the shuttering down – the lads would say, "What was it like? Did it turn out all right? Was there any cement loss?" When we first started off, I remember we did the first four down at the bottom of the crypt. We struck it out, and it was, to my way of thinking, beautiful. It was snow-white and it stood out lovely. That was the wall as you came out of the crypt to go up the staircase. That was the first bit of white concrete we did in the cathedral. We had trials before that to get the mix right, we had a bit of a mock-up, played around with it.

'All the white concrete was mixed on the site. The grey concrete was supplied by Readymix. So the white concrete was completely controlled on the site. Normally, the procedure was that we had the job ready for concreting and I'd say to the Engineer, "We're going to concrete such and such tomorrow", and he'd say, "Right, I'll be there", and one would watch the pour and the other would watch it going into the mould. It was monitored from start to finish.'

The main problem they had to face was cement draining out through the joints in the shuttering. If this happened, the face of the concrete would be spoiled, the wood graining of the shutters would not be accurately reproduced in the concrete and the aggregate would appear on the surface. On other kinds of structure, this might not be very important, but, if it happened here, it was a disaster. So ways had to be found of preventing it.

'First of all, we found we were losing cement because we weren't getting a tight joint right round the wall, when we were bolting one section of shuttering to another. For the initial pour, you put a kicker round the bottom, clamp your shutters on, strike them up, pour the concrete. So the only place you could lose concrete in that case would be at the bottom, where the join is, or at the sides. This was our biggest problem to start with. The way we got over that was by introducing a rubber cushion, so that when the shutter was clamped to the existing concrete, the rubber would stop the leakage.

'The other thing was that you had to have a very good monitoring system from your supervisor and monitoring

Checking concrete after the shuttering had been removed. The men in the picture are from left to right: . . . Nelson; Dick Sidwick; Jock Rutt-ledge.

foreman, to make sure that the joiner who was doing that particular job tightened the bolts up when the pour was going on. His job was to check that the bolts were tight and, if there was the slightest sign of a leakage, to stop it immediately. You only had to lose an egg-cup full and a little bit of facing would be gone.

'The shutters were made so that you could use them as many times as possible, but we found that with the weather changing from wet to dry the shuttering would shrink. We had quite a few problems about that. Then there was the shuttering distorting. Sometimes we had to take the shutters apart after using them only two or three times and re-cramp them. In summer we found we had to put the shutters in water and let them float in it, to keep them tight. That was another little trick we discovered. Of course, they were quite big shutters, and we found that, if we made a polythene pond up on the scaffold and let the shutter float in that overnight, it was all right to use the next morning. I'm giving away a lot of trade secrets.'

Jock Ruttledge had direct responsibility for the shuttering.

'It was faced up with Russian redwood, which was specially chosen because of its quality of transmitting its grain on to concrete. The shutters were made in near enough 8 ft. by 4 ft. panels – there is a metric size, but it escapes me at the moment – and they were modulated, so that they plumbed up, one above the other, as the job grew.

'You had to be extremely accurate. There were no tolerances. It was either right or wrong. Every piece of shuttering that was erected was checked by the Resident Engineer himself for accuracy and for quality. And the Clerk of Works inspected it, too. If the white concrete wasn't 100% perfect when the shuttering was taken down, there was no way they would allow us to doctor it up. We could have made it so that you wouldn't have seen it, but as soon as the shutters were stripped they were there to inspect and, if it wasn't up to standard, it was out. They knocked it down. This only happened once, to my knowledge. Only one panel was taken down.'

With a job as complicated as this, it was no good the joiners being super-accurate and super-careful unless the drawings they were working to were equally perfect. And Jock Ruttledge paid a special tribute to the people who made the drawings.

'The setting out on the job was excellent. It was absolutely out of this world. We had a drawing office on the site and the name of the man in charge of it was House, Andrew House. He was the man who got the architect's drawings and he used to break it up for the joiners' shop to make the shutters.

'But what a lot of people don't realise about this is that a lot of the shutters that went into this job were made on the scaffolding as we went up. They couldn't be made in the joiners' shop, because to get the correct angles we used to work from string lines. These were strung at the right pitch and then we took the measurements of the boards that had to be cut for the shapes and made the shutters up there on the scaffold, and fixed them. Because of the shape of the building – diminishing as it went up – they were using the same shuttering panels all the way up, but making them smaller all the time. Sometimes it was a terrific problem, because of the wind, especially when we were working on the fleche. I had seven or eight men for that, working to string lines or plumb bobs.

'Some days on the ground there wasn't enough wind to blow out a candle, but once you got up to 200 feet it could be very different. Now and again, I had to call a halt. I said, "Right, it's too bad, down, it's a waste of time." When we got down – we had other work on the ground we could get on with – we communicated with the office to tell them about our problem and they wouldn't believe it. They said, "No way." So we told them to go up and see for themselves.

'I can't remember any bad accidents, though. Minor things, you know, like chaps carrying shutters and tripping, that sort of thing. You always get that.'

As he remembers it, the unusually high standards took a little while to get used to, even for first-class men.

'To be honest, until they got into a system and a pattern, the men were under a certain amount of tension, because they were frightened of getting it wrong, of having their work taken down, and they made every effort that was humanly possible to make sure that it didn't happen. But I think when it really got going people were more relaxed.'

With forty years' experience in the construction industry behind him, Jock Ruttledge felt able to say that Clifton Cathedral was 'the happiest job I was ever associated with', and Alan Mansfield used much the same kind of language. By asking them why they felt this was so, one learns a great deal about the recent history of the building industry.

To begin with, there is no doubt that the cathedral contract had a Site Agent much above the usual level, a man with an exceptional talent for getting the best out of men and for creating a pleasant working atmosphere. About fifty men were working on the site at any given time, and Mr Barnes, the Agent, made sure that every one of them was shown right at the beginning how his job fitted into the project as a whole. Jock Ruttledge remembers him with great affection and respect.

'Each man who came on the job would be brought to his office and would have a cup of tea and a cigarette and a general chat about the job. Mr Barnes had a model made and he used to give each man a run-down on the job and on the various phases of it. He'd tell the chap he was interviewing what was expected of him and what he'd be doing. This wasn't just a ten-minute chat. It was really something. He had this model and he said, "You'll be here, you'll do this and that, and this is what you'll be using, and while you're doing that, this, that and the other will be going on."

'Mr Barnes was a one-off and so was the Clerk of Works, Mr Murray.'

There seems to be some disagreement between Mr Ruttledge and Mr Mansfield as to whether the men employed on the contract were, in fact, quite as hand-picked as John Laing and Co. made out. In Mr Ruttledge's view. 'They were not picked. I understand men were sent along as they became available.' But Mr Mansfield was certain the quality of the labour force was much above the average. 'The carpenters were our best carpen-

A Laing's group on the Cathedral contract. The men in the picture are, from left to right: Mike Dymianczik; Dick Sidwick; Ted Jones; . . . Nelson; Mr Murray (Clerk of Works); Jock Ruttledge.

ters. The young apprentices, the young tradesmen we had, were all good tradesmen. They were there because we just couldn't afford not to have them. We couldn't afford too many mistakes.'

The truth may be that most of the men were pretty good to start with, but that working on this particular job made them better. Whatever the cynics may say, people still do respond to a pleasant working atmosphere and to high standards of performance. All that Clifton Cathedral did – and it is a very big all – was to prove the point, and in that sense it was a notable laboratory of industrial relationships.

But work on it began ten years ago and conditions in the construction industry may well have deteriorated since then. Alan Mansfield felt that in terms of manpower the job was probably carried out at the last possible moment and since then it has become steadily more difficult to find men of the quality required. Apprentices nowadays rarely receive the all-round training that was once taken for granted.

'Young tradesmen just don't have experience in the different lines of the trade that they should have. You might get one particular contract where there's a lot of shuttering involved. The young carpenter works on the shuttering, and then he comes off that and goes on to houses, where you find he probably hasn't ever hung a door or fixed a flight of stairs. I said to a young chap, 22 or 23, "Put that flight of stairs up and do so and so", and he said, "I haven't ever put up a flight of stairs", and that was a properly apprenticed carpenter.

'You'd be surprised, especially with the bigger companies. The ideal company to provide training for young apprentices today would be a small builder, putting up two or three houses a year. A lad would be bound to get a variety of work that way.'

The real cause of the decline in all-round skill, in Alan Mansfield's opinion, was the bonus scheme that came in soon after the Second World War. He himself was only an apprentice at the time, but he remembers the situation very well.

'The general feeling in the industry then was the joiners didn't want to know the bonus, but the bricklayers and the plumbers and the plasterers, they did. So that's what happened, the bonus scheme came in, and everyone was out to get the repetition jobs. You could hang eight doors a day and do quite well. I know carpenters who could hang sixteen doors a day and that was all they did. Can you imagine that, sixteen doors a day? Our own company used to hand over in the region of thirty-two houses a week – and one house has a lot of doors.'

The ordinary bonus system would have been disastrous on the Clifton Cathedral contract, where quality of workmanship was all-important. So all the men were put on what was known as a standing bonus, a guaranteed bonus. This meant that they had no need to go for quantity in order to make the kind of money they were used to. They could concentrate on doing the job as it ought to be done and, for a first-class craftsman, this was a memorable experience, a return to the good old days.

After the shell of the cathedral was finished and the shuttering problems were over, Jock Ruttledge went over to making the joinery and fittings. Here, too, everything was of the best.

'The joinery consisted of the finest hardwood you could get, with oak and ash doors. It was all good quality joinery and the ironmongery was the best there was. It was wonderful working with material like that. I've worked on jobs before and since, like hospitals, where we did use good quality timber, but this was really good.'

All the joinery apprentices Laing had during those three years worked for a spell on the cathedral, so that they could understand just what was meant by first-class standards of workmanship. Whether this was cruel or kind is an open question. The construction industry nowadays offers very few opportunities of the Clifton kind, and to be compelled to spend the rest of one's life doing work of an inferior quality must be a frustrating experience.

Alan Mansfield and his family are, as it happens, Catholics and they go to the cathedral at Clifton from time to time. Alan Mansfield naturally casts an expert eye over it, to see how time and the weather are dealing with it. On the whole, he finds everything very satisfactory. All the careful planning and good workmanship have paid off. Some staining is noticeable on the external concrete, but no cracking. The only major problem seems to be the underfloor electric heating, which has turned out to be very expensive, mainly because it takes a long time for the heat to come through the floor slab.

'The company,' said Alan Mansfield, 'is very pleased with the cathedral, even though they tell us they never made any money from the job. But they always tell us that. I'm sure a lot of good ideas came out of it, though. We're doing the new concert hall in Cardiff, and the company's still picking the cathedral's brains for that.'

If we were able to talk to the men who built Salisbury and Durham and Wells and all the other medieval cathedrals, we should certainly find out as much as the conversations with Jock Ruttledge and Alan Mansfield revealed about Clifton. Builders are essentially adaptable and ingenious people. Unexpected problems are always turning up and they have to be solved quickly as they come along. Sometimes the answers are wrong, especially where new materials and new construction techniques are involved, and future generations of architects and builders have to spend a lot of time and money putting things right. Not infrequently, the men engaged on the project know perfectly well that they are being compelled to do inferior work and that the results can only be bad, bad for the customer, bad for themselves and bad for the public which has to look at a botched job year after year.

None of this is true for Clifton Cathedral, where the brief was altogether exceptional. 'This building,' said the Bishop, 'has got to last for at least 300 years', a demand which was never made of the medieval cathedral builders. We should not, perhaps, take the Bishop too literally. All he was really insisting on was that the new cathedral should have real stamina and that it should cost as little as possible to run and maintain. But nobody ever speaks of a new office block in such terms. If it gives reasonable service for fifty years, it will probably be reckoned to have done well and the owners will have got their money back, and a profit into the bargain. Whether the people who have to use the building will be satisfied with it is another matter. In nine cases out of ten nowadays, the architect and the construction company have no idea whatever who is going to occupy a new building. It is simply a building for letting. The men who actually put it up and fit it out have no interest in it. It has simply been a job, a source of income.

Clifton was a construction worker's dream, something to be proud of, something different, something to identify oneself with, something to remember. It is the shame of our times that so little work is like this now and, in this sense, the atmosphere created during the three years of the building of this modern cathedral belongs to a past age.

Listen, for instance, to Alan Mansfield talking about the hexagonal beams supporting the balcony over the font.

'This was an interesting job, because, to make the balcony look level, we had to construct the beams with a camber in them to give them the appearance of being straight. The camber was about two inches across both ways of the balcony. This meant that all the intersecting beams on the hexagonal had to be constructed out of plumb, to give them the appearance of being plumb. On a 3 ft. deep beam, this is quite a difficult operation, especially since all the beams over the font had to be concreted in one go. Next time you visit the cathedral, have a look at this and you will see what I am trying to explain.'

Without in any way disparaging the achievements of the men who designed and built the medieval cathedrals, it is fair to say that nothing they did was more difficult or more ingenious than the task Alan Mansfield has just described. But, without the record he has provided, how many people, now or in a hundred years' time, would have realised the technical problems with which this team of late twentieth century construction workers had to grapple? And how interesting and useful we should find similar accounts from the thirteenth and fourteenth century equivalents of Alan Mansfield and Jock Ruttledge.

Chapter Two   Making and selling furniture

For more than three hundred years, London has been the main centre of the furniture industry. The workshops have been of two kinds. First, during the seventeenth and eighteenth centuries, cabinet-makers, chair-makers, carvers, gilders and upholsterers producing for the expensive end of the trade and serving well-to-do customers from all over Britain. And second, from the early nineteenth century onwards, what can be fairly described as manufacturing, meeting the requirements of the rapidly expanding middle class for furniture of reasonably good quality and modest prices. Broadly speaking, the seventeenth and eighteenth century workshops made furniture to order, while the nineteenth operated in a much bigger market and was based on standardised products. There was, even in the early Victorian period, a great deal of specialisation and sub-contracting. A large firm might assemble, finish and sell furniture, but the components could be made up by several sub-contractors, often on a garden shed or backroom basis.

The railways revolutionised furniture-making, as they did many other consumer industries. In the days of Chippendale and Sheraton, sending furniture to customers all over the British Isles was a difficult and expensive business, only worth bothering about because the price was high enough to absorb the transport costs and because the quality of the goods was exceptional. At that time, and for much of the nineteenth century too, ordinary people employed local carpenters to provide them with such furniture as they had. It was solidly built and it had to last a long time, being normally passed down from one generation to another. The mass-production furniture industry was brought into being by three factors – cheap imported timber, steam-driven woodworking machinery, railways and a population which was growing faster than the traditional system of craftsmen workshops could supply it with goods.

In the mid-nineteenth century, the London furniture-makers,

at all levels of skill, elegance and price, were concentrated around Tottenham Court Road and in the East End, chiefly Shoreditch and Bethnal Green. There were also a number of firms in and around Edmonton, where imported timber could be easily brought up the River Lea from the London docks. Some of the largest twentieth century furniture firms, like B. and I. Nathan, began as cabinet-makers in the Edmonton area. The Jewish element in the London furniture industry was strong throughout the nineteenth century and is still important. Cabinet-making, like tailoring, was a trade which could be carried on at home, and both occupations were frequently characterised by wretchedly poor working conditions and by scandalous exploitation. A study of the invaluable Post Office Trade Directories for the period 1850–1950 reveals a high proportion of obviously Jewish names among both the furniture and timber firms in East and North London. Many of them had their premises demolished or severely damaged in Second World War air-raids and the national pattern of the industry developed in quite a different way after the war. London lost much of its former pre-eminence and new manufacturing centres in the provinces took over an increasing amount of the market.

Herbert Vaughan's family had a furniture business in the East End. He himself is now retired and lives in Kent, but one of his sons is still in the business. His reminiscences show just how precarious the trade was, with so many people trying to make a living in it and profit margins so small.

His father, also Herbert Vaughan, ran away from home and went to sea. When he eventually returned to England in 1906, he decided to try his hand as a chairmaker. A number of his relations were in various branches of the furniture business and he started up on his own in Bethnal Green, in a small rented workshop and with very little capital. He assembled chair frames, buying the legs and rails ready-machined from the timber merchants, who mass-produced them. It was not very difficult to establish himself, despite the cut-throat competition. The people with power were the firms who bought chair frames and, in his son's words, 'he found out how much they were paying for their frames and did them 2d. cheaper. That gave him a start.'

The only parts Mr Vaughan Senior had to make for himself were the dowels, the pieces of round wooden rod that were driven into bored holes and used to fix the parts of the chair frame together. 'Dowels were made with a dowel plate, that's to say, a piece of metal with a $\frac{3}{8}$ in. hole in it. You got a piece of wood and drove it through the plate. This produced a dowel. You had to make your own dowels. You couldn't buy them at that time.'

Timber store of a typical East End furniture workshop in the Thirties.

The system was still the same when Herbert Vaughan Junior went to work with his father in 1923, when he was fourteen. He was so anxious to start the job that he was there the day after he left school, travelling in every day from Southend, where his family lived. The previous year the business had been moved from 1A Hoxton Street, to 56 Church Street, off Shoreditch High Street.

'It was a very big building. We used to let off part of the ground floor to a turner and twister, and part of the first floor was another chairmaker's. He was a small chair-maker. He used to make only Queen Anne chairs, dining chairs. At that time we were partly chair frame makers, as we had been originally, but we were also a trade mill, making parts for other chair-makers and cabinet-makers in the district.

'We had about 18 men working for us. It was a very poorly paid trade. In those days, an experienced man got about £2 10s. a week. Might have gone up to £3. That was for $52\frac{1}{2}$ hours. 8 to 7, Monday to Friday and 8 to 1 on Saturdays. An hour off for lunch.'

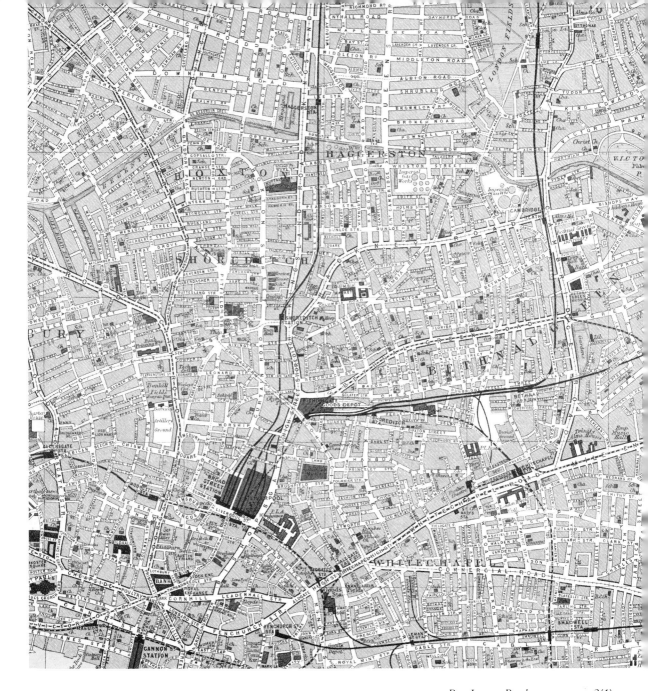

Furniture workshops in the East End, early 1920s

The figure against each street represents the total number of workshops and the figure in brackets the number with obviously Jewish names.

Allenby Road	*1(1)*	
Amberley Street	*1(1)*	
Arline Street	*1(0)*	
Arnos Road	*1(0)*	
Assembly Passage	*1(1)*	
Audrey Street	*1(0)*	
Austin Street	*10(9)*	
Bacon Street	*4(4)*	
Bedford Street	*1(1)*	

Ben Jonson Road	*2(1)*
Bethnal Green Road	*18(9)*
Bishops Road	*2(0)*
Bishop's Row	*1(0)*
Bonner Street	*1(0)*
Boundary Street	*7(2)*
Brick Lane	*29(23)*
Brook Street	*1(0)*
Broomsbury Street	*1(1)*
Brown Yard, Temple Street	*1(0)*

Brunswick Street	4(3)
Buckhurst Street	1(1)
Busby Street	2(2)
Buxton Street	8(7)
Cable Street	2(2)
Calvert Avenue	2(2)
Cambridge Road	1(1)
Chambord Street	2(2)
Charles Street	1(1)
Cheshire Street	1(1)
Chicksand Street	1(1)
Chiltern Street	2(1)
Christian Street	3(3)
Church Court	1(1)
Church Row	2(1)
Church Street	11(11)
Club Row	5(3)
Coate Street	1(1)
Coke Street	1(1)
Columbia Market	3(2)
Columbia Road	28(19)
Columbia Street	1(1)
Commercial Road	4(3)
Commercial Street	1(1)
Cosser Street	1(0)
Cremer Street	1(1)
Cutler Street	1(1)
Cygnet Street	1(1)
Dock Street	1(0)
Dunloe Street	5(3)
Ebor Street	1(1)
Elder Street	1(1)
Exmouth Street	1(1)
Ezra Street	4(2)
Finch Street	1(1)
Florida Street	1(0)
Fountain Street	2(2)
Fournier Street	1(1)
Francis Street	1(0)
French Place, Shoreditch	1(0)
Fuller Road	1(1)
Fuller Street	1(1)
Gayneland Road	1(0)
Gibraltar Walk	22(13)
Globe Road	8(5)
Goldsmith's Row	10(3)
Gossett Street	5(2)
Granby Street	1(1)
Great Cambridge Street	3(2)
Great Eagle Street	1(1)
Great Peare Street	6(6)
Great Pell Street	2(2)
Green Street	3(2)
Greenfield Court	1(1)

Greenfield Street	1(1)
Grimsby Street	1(1)
Gun Street	2(2)
Hackney Road	37(20)
Half Moon Passage	1(1)
Hanbury Street	4(4)
Hare Street	19(16)
Hassard Street	3(2)
Henna Street	2(2)
Hocker Street	12(11)
Hollybush Gardens	1(0)
Houndsditch Road	1(0)
Hows Street	2(1)
Hulton Street	1(1)
Joan Street	1(1)
Jubilee Street	1(1)
Kay Street	1(1)
Kerbela Street	2(2)
Kingsland Road	26(17)
Laburnum Grove	1(1)
Laburnum Street	1(1)
Lark Row	1(1)
Little Peare Street	1(1)
Mansfield Street	1(0)
Mansford Road	2(1)
Mansford Street	1(0)
Mansworth Court	1(1)
Margaret Place	1(0)
Marlin Road	1(0)
Mile End Road	7(3)
Mount Street	6(5)
Newlyn Street	1(1)
Oatley Road	1(1)
Old Bethnal Green Road	1(0)
Old Ford Road	1(0)
Old Ford Street	2(0)
Old Montague Street	2(2)
Old Nichol Street	1(0)
Osborne Street	1(1)
Oxford Street	1(1)
Pearson Street	2(0)
Pedley Street	2(2)
Pelham Street	2(2)
Peter Street	2(2)
Plumber's Row	1(1)
Pollard Row	1(0)
Prince's Court	4(4)
Printbury, Print Place	1(1)
Pritchard's Road	1(0)
Rapley Place	2(1)
Ravenscroft Street	7(4)
Ravenshill Street	1(0)
Roan Horse Yard	5(1)

Robert Court	1(0)
Robinson Road	1(0)
Rupert Place	1(1)
St George's Street	1(1)
St Peter's Street	1(0)
Sale Street	1(1)
Satchwell Street	1(0)
Sclater Street	5(5)
Sewardstone Road	1(0)
Sheffie Place	1(1)
Shepherd Street	1(1)
Shoreditch High Street	2(1)
Sidney Street	1(1)
Spital Street	1(1)
Stamford Place	1(0)
Teesdale Street	11(5)
Temple Street	9(3)
Tuilerie Street	3(0)
Turin Street	2(1)
Umberston Street	1(1)
Vallance Road	3(3)
Vandon Street	1(1)
Virginia Road	16(14)
Waltham Place	1(0)
Watney Street	1(1)
Wentworth Street	1(1)
Weymouth Terrace	5(2)
Whitechapel Road	2(2)
Willow Court	1(0)
Winchester Street	3(2)

A pre-war survival in Weymouth Terrace.

Herbert Junior began work under the supervision of a Jewish employee, whom he remembers as 'Morrie'.

'I started off doing shaving. I didn't think much of that. Too much like hard work – involved a lot of sandpapering. I progressed from there to working a planing machine. We'd just bought a new 32 in. planing machine – the old man must have made some money, during the War I think – and I took that up. I was taught how to use it, how to sharpen the cutters. You have what's basically a roller with four slots in it, in which you insert four 32 in. knives. It was belt-driven, three speeds. If you wanted to change the speeds, you just knocked the belt off and pushed it with a stock on the other end.

'The machines were installed in the yard with a corrugated iron roof constructed over it. Nowadays you've got to have the right temperature to work, it was pretty cold in the winter. The whole thing was cold. We had the planing machine, we had three bandsaws, one 36 in. with phosphor-bronze bearings, and two 32 in. One was in the front shop and the other one was set behind the first one. They were just off the yard. Timber used to be taken into the bandsaws there for machining. Over the back we had two spindle-moulding machines, any shape you liked, the man made his own cutters. We were working for the trade, so whatever customers wanted, we had to be prepared to do.

'It was mostly very short runs. Our customers were very small firms. They didn't have any machines of their own and they relied on us to do their machine work. The machine work that is done today in a cabinet factory was then done by us.

'We had two fretsaws, and they were kept going all day long. I had two brothers, and one of them did nothing else but fretsawing, because in those days decorations on all sorts of furniture were by means of frets. You remember the early days of wireless? Those cabinets all had fret-cut fronts to them.'

In 1923 good quality plywood had not yet arrived and the sides of bottoms of drawers still had to be made from solid wood. A drawer-bottom is only about a quarter of an inch thick, so that cutting it and putting it on the planing machine was, as Herbert Vaughan well remembers, 'a very tricky business, because it could easily break up and go to smithereens.'

The cutting of curved drawer-fronts was an equally skilled and potentially troublesome affair. 'A cabinet-maker would get a number of pieces of 1 inch thick mahogany, glue them together into a block, and then mark the shape he wanted on the top. The blocks were then taken to a machinist for cutting with the bandsaw. The cabinet-makers were very fussy about the quality of the work they had done. One customer in particular, Mr Eisenstein, wouldn't let anyone but me cut his drawer fronts.'

Getting orders was a pretty murderous affair. On the frame-making side, for instance: 'We would quote 18s. 6d. for a settee and two armchairs and if we wanted the order we had to do it for 18s. 3d. It was so cut-throat that we never really had any money. My father used to wait until he got the summons in for the rates. Our rates were £56 a quarter, and it cost us 1s. for the summons before we paid it. It was worth it, because you got the use of the £56 for that much longer. You just hadn't got the money to do it any other way. And it was like that right up to 1939.

'When war was declared all our customers disappeared, they didn't want to know, and we didn't know where they'd gone to, but our creditors knew us alright, so they were after us. Fortunately, by that time, we had become a limited company, but my father was still the leaseholder and therefore he was our landlord. As our landlord he distrained for the rent, so that when it came to the creditors chasing us for money they were too late, because Mr H. Vaughan had distrained the rent on H.

Vaughan Limited. That was how it was. But we managed to keep going, and we kept the men in work.'

The firm had an office, but it was always regarded as a very part-time affair. Everybody, the Vaughan family included, worked at the bench and the paper-work was looked after in odd moments. The system, even so, was efficient.

'The way you used to cost up the work, the mill work, was this. You had a notebook, and you kept a record of how many cuts you did, say, 50 straight cuts at $\frac{1}{2}$d. each, or two dozen heads or back legs at 1d. each. Anything rather difficult, like a long settee top would probably be costed at 2d. You put it all down in your book and that was collected up and the invoices were made up from the books each man kept who operated the machine. The man wasn't paid by what was in his book. That didn't have anything to do with it. His wages were his wages. What was in his book was what you charged the customer.'

Accidents were not common. Mr Vaughan has no memory of people losing fingers in the machines, although he himself has still got 'a flat big toe', as a result of a heavy plank once falling on it. The Factory Inspectors paid occasional visits, 'but you didn't really take any notice of them. They'd send you a letter and tell you what you ought to do, but they weren't really troublesome.'

And then the war came. 'Everybody disappeared. My father joined the River Emergency Service; my uncle, who had joined the company by then, went up north in a munitions factory; my two brothers went to the Royal Mint, and I carried on with one or two men myself, doing frame-making. By that time most people had closed down and timber was difficult to get hold of, but I carried on on my own. I was travelling up from Southend, about an hour and a quarter's journey, and I found this a bit too much. So we had a flat in the factory. My wife and I moved into the flat, and we stayed there until the anti-aircraft fire got a bit too noisy. Then we moved down into the mill, which had no windows to it, only had openings on one side, and we made ourselves a shelter in one corner. We built up a pile of sacks of firewood here, right the way round, with a bed in the corner, and slept there in the corner.'

The bombs finally drove them out of Church Street.

'Christmas 1940, the first very heavy bombing of London. I remember walking through all the glass in the side streets. My father came back to the factory after night duty with the Emergency Service. There'd been a land-mine dropped and it landed in the toilet of all places. It stood upright, so it didn't explode, but they were dropping incendiaries and, because of the land-mine being there, the local authorities wouldn't let the old man back into the building. We had a flat roof, his flat was above the flat roof, in other words you could walk out of his back door onto the flat roof and he could have saved the building if he had been allowed to go in. But he wasn't allowed to go in, and it was burnt down. The land-mine didn't explode. But the building didn't exist.

'I started up again on the opposite side of the road in the back street, in Whitby Street, in premises which had been a chair-maker's. Fortunately, we didn't lose all our machines because we'd taken a number of them away and put them down in my wife's father's garage. Surplus machines we weren't using, you see.'

Soon after that, Mr Vaughan went away to the Army. His father managed as well as he could, and somehow kept the business going, getting odds and ends of timber where he could and doing most of the work himself. The bombers eventually got Whitby Street, too, and there had to be another move, this time to a four-room rented workshop in Brick Street. When Mr Vaughan Junior returned in 1946, the firm had begun making chairs under the Utility Furniture scheme. Since then, it has enjoyed prosperity of a kind never even dreamt of before the

At the bench in Hackney.

33

war, with new premises in Witney Street and the next generation of the family in charge. An experienced machinist now asks for and gets £120 a week, which makes Mr Vaughan think wryly of the £2 10s. paid in 1923.

In some ways, he reckons the trade hasn't changed very much.

'There was plenty of shoddy work in the Twenties and Thirties and there still is. The joints aren't proper joints. They put the side up against a wall and knock the front against it and hope for the best. In those days, yes, frames were often made out of packing cases. Arms, you could put a piece of 5 in. packing-case material there. They weren't all that bad then, even the bad ones, better than the bad ones today. I mean, some of the bad ones today are really bad. You see, they've got to bash them up.'

There are some interesting things to be said about timber, too.

'Before the war, the only timber used for making frames was Canadian birch, the better quality being from Halifax and the second quality from St Johns. They were very good timbers. The price would vary from 2s. 3d. to 2s. 6d. a cube. Now, since the war, there's nothing else but beech. The cheap firms use English beech. It tends to warp, and gets a bit knotty. We only use Continental beech ourselves, the best's Yugoslavian. Yugoslavia's got a bit out of the price range now, so we're using Romanian, French and a bit of Swedish. Before the war we only had one consignment of European beech. We were used to having pieces 6 in. and 8 in. wide. This came in about 30 in. wide. It was perfect, perfect, not a blemish anywhere. Wonderful stuff.'

Those golden days, alas, have gone and much of the timber that goes into even expensive furniture nowadays would have made an old-time craftsman drop his tools in horror.

For many years, a number of the leading London furniture stores had their own workshops, where very high quality work was carried out. Whiteleys was a case in point. Mr J. Dudman began a five year apprenticeship there as an upholsterer in the early Twenties, when he was fourteen.

'In my first year I was more or less an errand boy, visiting warehouses in the East End of London, procuring patterns of trimmings and so on for customers' furniture that was being re-upholstered. In the second year I was upholstering what was called 'small furniture', such as loose seats. In the third year I moved on to suites, and in the fourth year I became an improver. In the year I completed my apprenticeship, the fifth year, I was reckoned to be able to do practically everything.'

Whiteleys used only the best materials at that time. Their names run off Mr Dudman's tongue like a poem: 'Mohair

Velvets; Saddlebags; Goat Skins; Hides; many Blue/Gold and Blue/Silver Damasks with Chinese designs; Tapestries; Silk Brocades.'

And, for such beautiful things, nothing but first-class treatment was possible.

'The workmanship was excellent. Nothing was mass-produced. There was no foam rubber or patent springing. Fillings were horse-hair or fibres, and all the springs were sewn on separately. All the cushion interiors were either feather or down.'

It was a big factory, with good working conditions, including plenty of daylight. Twenty-four upholsterers, two improvers and two apprentices were employed there, together with five women machinists. The work was supervised by a foreman and an under-foreman. From Monday to Friday the hours were 8 to 5.30, and on Saturdays from 8 to 12.30, forty seven in all.

The apprentices started at 12s. 6d. a week, rising to £2 10s. in the fourth year. Once out of an apprenticeship, piece work was the rule, at 2s. 6d. an hour. There were no paid holidays, not even Bank Holidays. Employees were rewarded only for the work they actually did. These were the days when one could buy an upholstered fireside chair at Whiteleys for £1 3s. 6d., a three-piece suite at from £19 19s. 0d. to the most expensive one in the catalogue at £145 10s. 0d. This one was covered in silk brocade.

'On completion of one's apprenticeship,' Mr Dudman remembers, 'one had to leave to gain experience. So I went to work for such firms as James Shoolbred in Tottenham Court Road, Waring and Gillows of Hammersmith and John Barkers of Kensington, not forgetting Harland and Wolf of Southampton, where I did work on the Cunard liner, 'Berengaria', which was a German liner handed over for reparation after the 1914–18 War.'

The 'improvers' mentioned by Mr Dudman were much sought after by employers, because, although they were skilled men, they were not paid the full adult wage. Mr Jack Byrne's experiences were fairly typical. His apprenticeship was with Murdock's Pianos, in Lewisham, South-East London, and during those years, the early Twenties, he did rather less well than Mr Dudman at Whiteleys. For the first year he received 10s. a week and after that it was 'whatever one was able to get.'

Once out of his apprenticeship, he went as an improver to Morris Morris, who had a small cabinet-making business in Shoreditch. Here there were four men, in addition to Mr Morris and his two sons. They made four bedroom suites a week and sold them to the wholesale trade. He stayed with Morris for eight years, from 1927 to 1935.

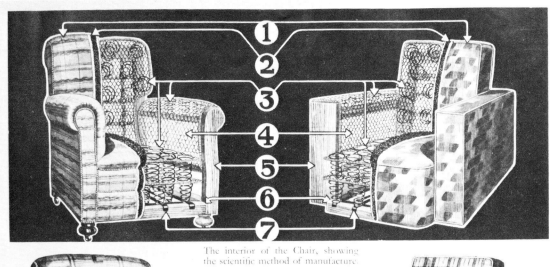

The interior of the Chair, showing
the scientific method of manufacture.
The materials used are the best of their
kind, clean, wholesome and hygienic.

A Conventional Club Chair.
Style "Y"

Style "Z" in a typical all-over covering
of appropriate modern pattern.

Companion to Style "Y"
—the wing model.

Style "Z" an alternative scheme—a contemporary
vogue—the dual patterned or toned covering.

Wm. WHITELEY Ltd., QUEEN'S ROAD & WESTBOURNE GROVE, LONDON, W.2. Phone: BAYSWATER 1234

AN AMBASSADOR OF WHITELEY'S UPHOLSTERY VALUES . . . . . .

THE WHITELEY EASY CHAIR

This chair has been designed to meet a popular demand at a popular price. Thousands have been sold and have given universal satisfaction. An alternative modern style at the same price as the conventional type is a recent introduction. Great care has been taken in so designing it that it will give the utmost comfort, being high enough in the back to take the head and deep enough in the seat to give restful ease.

Great care has been taken also in the selection of the materials that go to its manufacture and in the quality of the workmanship, so as to produce a chair that will wear for years.

It can be supplied in various Tapestries, Damasks and Velours, and the value of the covering governs the price of the completed article.

Price of the various ranges will be sent on application.

PRICE FOR CHAIRS IN 'A' RANGE £4 19 6   PRICE FOR CHAIRS IN 'B' RANGE £5 10 0   PRICE FOR CHAIRS IN 'C' RANGE £6 6 0

The Companion Chair, the "WHITELEY WING" Easy Chair

at the following prices:

PRICES FOR CHAIRS IN 'A' RANGE £5 17 6   PRICES FOR CHAIRS IN 'B' RANGE £6 7 6   PRICES FOR CHAIRS IN 'C' RANGE £7 5 0

In addition, this Wing Chair can be supplied in a special range of quality Velours for £7 17 6

THE FOUNDATION OF ITS COMFORT AND DURABILITY

Abridged details of the Sectional Drawings shown on other page:

1.—The outer covering of hard wearing Tapestry, Damask or Velour.
2.—The clean crisp curled Hair, giving Luxurious Ease.
3.—The best quality resilient Steel Springs, coppered to prevent rust.
4.—Strong wire mesh giving even distribution of strength.
5.—The strong Birch frame.
6.—The dowelled and glued joints.
7.—Steel Laths replace usual webbing, providing maximum comfort with great durability.

THE DIMENSIONS ARE:

Style 'Y'		Wing Easy Chair		Style 'Z'	
Width across arms	32 ins.	Depth of seat	24 ins.	Width across arms	32 ins.
Width between arms	20 „	Overall	31 „	Width between arms	20 „
Depth on bottom rail	29½ „	Height at back	34 „	Depth on bottom rail	29½ „
Depth of seat	22 „	Width over the wings	29 „	Depth of seat	22 „
Height to top of seat	14½ „	Width between the wings	18 „	Height to top of seat	14½ „
Extreme height	35 „			Extreme height	35 „

PAGE 30   Wm. WHITELEY Ltd., QUEEN'S ROAD & WESTBOURNE GROVE, LONDON, W.2. Phone: BAYSWATER 1234

'An Ambassador of Whiteley's upholstery values'. The Whiteley Easy Chair, c. 1930.

'My first workshop,' he recalls, 'was a very small two-storey place in Brick Lane, Shoreditch. The firm expanded fairly quickly and moved its premises three times during the years I was with them, first to Virginia Road, Shoreditch, then to Brunswick Road, also in Shoreditch, and after that to Cambridge Heath. By the time I left Morris, I was earning the full rate of 1s. 8½d. an hour.'

This, one observes, was considerably less than Whiteleys paid their upholsterers, and the difference probably reflects two levels of trade. It is worth remembering, however, that the Morrises evidently understood their business and the market very well, because they continued to grow despite the economic depression which plagued Britain, like everywhere else, during the Twenties and Thirties. They made only bedroom furniture, always for wholesalers, and they kept their staff together in a period when many other firms had to contract or close altogether. 'I was never out of work' Mr Byrne recalls gratefully, and there were few people employed in the furniture trade then who could say as much.

Mr Bert Segal's family were cabinet-makers in the East End of London from 1912 to 1948. Their workshops were first in Curtain Road and then in Hackney Road. Mr Segal himself entered the trade 'not very willingly' in 1924, when he was fourteen.

'We worked from 8 in the morning to 7 in the evening, with what we called "ghosters" until 9 or 10 on Thursdays, so that work could be delivered to the factors in time for the week-end. One of the main firms we used to supply was C. and R. Light, of 54 Great Eastern Street. They had been owned by the same family for more than a century.

'We made chiefly reproduction furniture. In my early days in the Twenties it was Hepplewhite cabinets, needed for the gramophone boom, and later on we did radio cabinets and bedroom furniture. I still treasure a repro Chippendale dining suite we made in 1922. That was at a time when we were selling Lights a walnut bedroom suite for £5 and one in oak for £3 10s.

'Competition was fierce and wages were very low. My wage to begin with was only 7s. 6d. a week. In the Twenties the average wage for a craftsman was a shilling an hour. By the outbreak of war the union rate was 1s. 8d. an hour or £4 2s. 6d. a week, but this wasn't always paid. Trade Boards were set up to prevent starvation wages, but in times of high employment the rates they laid down were mostly ignored. However low the wages were, though, it was still better to work than to be on the dole. In 1934 the dole for a single person was 13s. 4d. a week.'

If catalogues are a fair guide, C. and R. Light must have done quite well out of their dealings with Segals and the other manufacturers who supplied them. 'Fine figured mahogany or walnut bedroom suites', comprising a dressing table, 5 ft. wardrobe, and '2 ft. 9 in. dwarf robe' were retailed at £65. In oak, the price was £52. One has to remember, however, that the factors, in this case C. and R. Light, had to carry the cost of warehousing the furniture, possibly for several months, and of transporting it to whoever eventually bought it. All the other overheads, such as printing and distributing catalogues and paying travellers, also fell on them. Furniture has always been an awkward, expensive commodity to stock and sell and, largely for that reason, the difference between wholesale and retail prices is considerable. Even so, to pay £5 for something selling at £65 was not bad going.

It is interesting to notice that another firm, Chippendale's Workshops, of 12–18 Hoxton Street, Shoreditch, was able to offer walnut bedroom suites for as little as £35 15s. 0d., by selling directly from their own workshops. 'Why,' asked their advertising slogan, 'pay more than workshop prices for your furniture?' and, in the hard-up Twenties and Thirties, that was an attractive proposition.

Light's, incidentally, did manufacture some furniture themselves. They were makers, as well as factors, but their prices naturally reflected the factoring aspect of the business.

It is worth mentioning, perhaps, that during the whole of the nineteenth century and until after the Second World War a high proportion of working-class families never bought any new furniture at all. Their homes were made habitable with bits and pieces picked up from second-hand shops and stalls and from the households of relations and acquaintances who had died. Light's, the Chippendale Workshops and the rest were catering for a largely middle-class trade, a middle-class which, it is true, was remarkably hard-pressed for money at its lower levels, but which reckoned to equip itself with new furniture once in a lifetime. The more prosperous type of skilled workman had similar tastes and ambitions and, in houses and furniture as in other things, the line between the British middle and artisan class was extremely difficult to draw in pre-war times. Nowadays it no longer exists.

One of the oldest and best-known firms among British furniture makers and furniture retailers is Heal and Son Ltd, of Tottenham Court Road. Established as an upholstery and bedding business in 1810, it subsequently broadened out to include other kinds of furniture and furnishings, concentrating on the top end of the market and acquiring an international reputation for innovative design and good workmanship, mainly as a result of the efforts of Sir Ambrose Heal, who became managing director in 1913, and his son, Christopher, a designer of exceptional talent.

Several times rebuilt and extended, Heal's extensive premises in Tottenham Court Road included both workshops and showrooms. In 1978, the firm ceased making furniture itself, but the manufacture of bedding continues, using much the same craftsman methods as a hundred years ago. It has survived and on the whole prospered by a sound instinct for adapting to new social and economic conditions and by controlling and modifying fashion as well as bowing to it.

Survival was not always easy. The early Thirties were especially difficult, and in 1932 the firm brought out a catalogue-for-the-times, with the title, *Nineteen Thirty-Two and All That*, 'illustrating the "New Type" furniture and furnish-

RUSSET OAK DINING ROOM FURNITURE

TABLE. No.C474; solid top; stretcher below; 6ft. long by 2ft. 6in. wide	£ 6. 15. 0.
SIDEBOARD. No.C1085; 2 drawers & 2 cupboards (1 *fitted with shelf*); underpart with stretcher; 4ft. 3in. long by 1ft. 2in. from back to front	10. 10. 0.
DINING CHAIRS. No.D1224; loose seats and backs covered in a modern tapestry; stuffed all hair . . (*See also page 5*) . . each	1. 15. 0.
ARM CHAIRS. No.D1224a ditto ditto ditto each	2. 10. 0.
BOOK-TABLE. No.C526; octagonal; 20in. by 20in. on top: 20in. high (*The same in dark oak £2. 12. 6; in weathered oak £3. 3. 0; in polished mahogany £3. 15. 0. Also in a number of other designs, sizes and woods.*)	2. 12. 6.
WALL MIRROR. No.C774a; russet oak frame; 3ft.6in. long by 1ft.4in. (*The same in unpolished oak £2. 5. 0; in dark oak £2. 10. 0.*)	2. 10. 0.
PICTURE. No.LG1508; 'The Mustard Field'; unpolished oak frame; (*The same in stained black frame £1. 12. 6; in painted frame £2. 5. 0.*)	1. 19. 6.
WALL-LIGHT SHADE. No.E2071; natural oiled paper; 16in by 12in.	10. 0.
REVERSIBLE RUG. No.F100; wool and hair; modern design in green, black and yellow on buff ground; Indian make; 6ft. long by 3ft. wide (*4ft. 6in. by 2ft. 3in. 17/6; 5ft. by 2ft. 6in. 19/6; 7ft. by 4ft. £2. 2. 0. & larger sizes*)	1. 8. 6.

Heal's: 'For these times of Economy'.

HEAL & SON LTD.   4   TOTTENHAM COURT ROAD, W.1

ings specially designed and made by Heal's for these times of economy.' It was well-made furniture without frills, destined for the most part for the younger sections of the middle class, with more taste than money and remarkably like the Government-controlled Utility range of the immediate post-war period, thirteen years later. In 1935, as the nation's fortunes improved, Heal's brought out a new range and a new catalogue, *Furniture for Better Times.*

Peter Hewitt came to Heal's in 1941, when the famous furniture business had been crippled by a chronic shortage of supplies of nearly everything a furniture maker needs. His father was a Heal's veteran, having been taken on as a post boy in 1909 and progressing rapidly from there to becoming a salesman in the Upholstery Department, where he remained with great success until the end of his working life.

Force of circumstances brought Peter Hewitt to Heal's.

'I was just about to leave school when the war started and they were calling people up to the Services at the age of 21. I was then 18, but everybody that I approached for a job said, "Well, this lad's going to be in the Services, so we don't really want him", and in the end I was really getting a bit desperate, and father happened to mention to one of our Directors here that I was getting desperate, and so he said, "Bring him up here, we'll take him."'

He spent a short time in the Carpet Department.

'There was a very nice polished floor and the walls were white, and the windows were open along the far side there, which at the moment are closed, and we had rolls of body carpet stacked one on top of the other in various colours – it was very bright, very cheerful – and down the centre of the room we had piles of rugs, the squares that you would flick back to

Heal's: 'Furniture for Better Times', 1935.

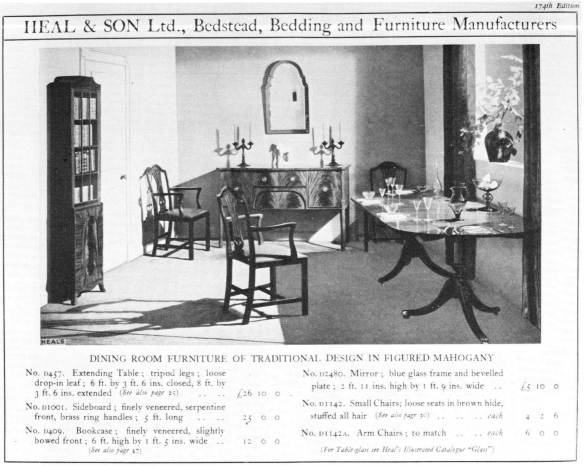

HEAL & SON Ltd., Bedstead, Bedding and Furniture Manufacturers

HEALS

DINING ROOM FURNITURE OF TRADITIONAL DESIGN IN FIGURED MAHOGANY

No. D457. Extending Table; tripod legs; loose drop-in leaf; 6 ft. by 3 ft. 6 ins. closed, 8 ft. by 3 ft. 6 ins. extended (*See also page 25*) .. .. £26 10 0 .

No. D1001. Sideboard; finely veneered, serpentine front, brass ring handles; 5 ft. long 25 0 0

No. D409. Bookcase; finely veneered, slightly bowed front; 6 ft. high by 1 ft. 5 ins. wide .. 12 0 0
(*See also page 47*)

No. D2480. Mirror; blue glass frame and bevelled plate; 2 ft. 11 ins. high by 1 ft. 9 ins. wide .. £5 10 0

No. D1142. Small Chairs; loose seats in brown hide, stuffed all hair (*See also page 30*) .. .. .. *each* 4 2 6

No. D1142A. Arm Chairs; to match .. .. *each* 6 0 0

(*For Table-glass see Heal's Illustrated Catalogue "Glass"*)

14   *For full list of Heal's Illustrated Catalogues, sent post free on request, see inside back cover.*

show the customers what they wanted. In the far corner there were rolls of lino, which we no longer sell today.'

The mention of the lino is interesting, because in those days lino was a fairly reliable indicator of income and status. The higher you rose in the social scale, the less likely you were to have lino. Mr Hewitt felt that Heal's customers in the early Forties were very different from Heal's customers today. 'They weren't,' he said, 'so affluent. We were down-trading rather more than we are today.'

There was an interesting reason for this. Until the outbreak of war, Heal's had a great many wealthy out-of-town customers. They were much more important than the local London people, but during the war they faded out of the picture, because Heal's could no longer supply them with the kind of goods they were used to. When the business was able to re-establish itself in something like its old style, a new type of wealthy customer began to reveal itself. 'They were Londoners, the people from St John's Wood and so on. They'd made a lot of money out of the war and they were quite a different kind of customer from the ones we had in 1939.'

Carpets, of course, were in very short supply – the position got much worse as the war progressed – and, as he well remembers, the young Peter Hewitt found himself in an embarrassing situation on one occasion.

'I had a customer come in while the manager was at lunch, and he walked round the showroom in front of these rolls of carpet. He started saying he would have that whole roll, 45 yards, whatever it was, at £2 a yard, and then he'd have the one beneath it, and then he'd have those four over there, and I thought, "This is marvellous" because I was on a commission, very basic, and I thought, "I'm doing very well." And then it appeared that he was almost prepared to buy the whole of the floor. It was another retailer. Supplies were so bad that he was prepared to pay our prices. I think we sold him two pieces, something like that.'

A few months later, he was transferred to the parachute factory which Heal's were running on the premises in Tottenham Court Road. A thousand girls were working there, on the third, fourth and fifth floors of the building. There was a small subsidiary factory at Market Harborough, also operated by Heal's, in part of Symington's corset factory. Peter Hewitt was drafted there, together with 'a Mr Treleven, who was a very clever man in bedding, but he was also very good at running a factory.' And after eleven months of that, Peter Hewitt went into the Army.

When he came back in 1947, the girls were still there and, until they were found other jobs, Heal's took on contracts to make raincoats and sandals. By 1950, the girls had all departed,

Heal's: War-time stock. The bulge in the roller-shutter, below the sign, 'Beds and Bedding', was the result of bomb-blast.

Heal's: Looking after the staff in wartime. The basement hostel for bombed-out families, decorated for a children's Christmas party.

43

*Heal's as a war-time parachute fac-
tory.*

the parachute/raincoat factory had become a furniture store
again, and Heal's were forging ahead with Utility furniture.

And, with the business returning to normal, Robin Hartley
arrived at Heal's, as a trainee in the Bedding Department. This
was in 1956. He is still there, and still in the Bedding Department, but in recent years he has added the post of Company
Archivist to his responsibilities, an agreeable task, which gives
him considerable historical perspective. The Fifties, as he
remembers them, were an exciting time at Heal's.

'There was always something new coming along, or indeed
new to me. We used to have new design parties every year,
where we had new designs of furniture in wood, and it was
nearly always to do with wood because wood was almost a new
fashion, because we couldn't get it during the War.

'I remember being absolutely horrified at the prices that we
were expected to ask for hand-made stuff, but it sold. In those
days – I'm going to sound like a frightful snob – you could tell a
customer's wealth by the way they were dressed, whereas
nowadays they might come in with bare feet and tatty jeans and

44

spend thousands. In those days you could look at their shoes and work your way up, and decide whether they could or couldn't afford what you were offering them.'

In pre-war days most people were almost afraid to come into Heal's – the prices terrified them – but with the advent of Utility furniture and price restrictions in the early Fifties the position changed, because Heal's weren't allowed to charge more than anybody else. That was when design and workmanship came to have a special importance. In that sense, Utility was probably good for Heal's.

In the Fifties, Sir Ambrose Heal was still alive and very much an influence on the business. He was an exceedingly strong-willed man, and there are many stories to illustrate this. Peter Hewitt called one of them to mind.

'Along the front of the Upholstery and Curtaining Department they had show stands with yard samples of fabrics, and the frames of those were painted black. Mr Anthony Heal, who was up and coming on the managerial side by this time, decided to brighten the place. He would have them painted white. And so they were stripped, repainted, left to dry, reassembled, and put back. Sir Ambrose came through, saw the white frames and immediately said they were to be painted black, back to their original colour. And so they were stripped, painted black, reassembled and Sir Ambrose was happy again.'

His staff were reckoned to be frightened of him, but Robin Hartley denies this.

'It wasn't really fear. It was utter respect. You didn't do anything if you thought he wouldn't like it. Again, if you wanted to move right or left you had to think, would Sir Ambrose like it, am I going to do the right thing? Is it right for Heal's, because we must keep our image of being a rather perfectionist firm, and frequently, of course, you couldn't move left or right because Sir Ambrose wouldn't have liked it, and he knew what was right. He'd known what was right since 1893 when he joined the firm.'

After he died, in 1959, there were some rapid changes, all of which would have seemed impossible a few months earlier. 'Suddenly,' Robin Hartley remembers, 'I didn't have to wear a black jacket and pin-striped trousers. We were allowed to wear lounge suits of a dark colour. We no longer had to come in through the front door and be inspected by Mr Chapman, the Apprentice Master, who could, if we were looking scruffy, send us home and not pay us until we came back looking not scruffy. He was in charge of all the younger people and he had a book and the clock that is in my office, under which he sat and by which he checked the time that you arrived.'

And there was the little matter of the canteens. In Peter Hewitt's words:

'We had two canteens. The factory was absolutely separate from the staff, as they were known. Continuing the story of the factories, in the plural, because we had our bedding factory, we also had our curtain factory and also had our carpet factory, and the cabinet factory on the premises, and there was a big division between the two, the factory and the staff. But in the Fifties, when Sir Ambrose died, then things started to change and they came closer together, and finally we closed the factory canteen and had just one staff canteen where everyone came very much closer together, which was a good thing, because this division hadn't been good, there had been a certain amount of animosity between the factory workers and the staff. Gradually this disappeared, and now you can say we are one unit.'

Some of the stories about Sir Ambrose are no doubt apocryphal. He is supposed, for instance, to have had the habit of standing near the entrance, watching for customers who had the appearance of not being the type Heal's required. When such an unfortunate came through the door, Sir Ambrose would lift his hand, as a signal for the commissionaire to come forward and escort the undesirable character firmly back to the pavement.

This, however, is fact, not legend.

'In 1923 Sir Ambrose decided that we ought to be a democracy so that the factory people were given a little council of their own, and were able to make suggestions as to what should or should not be done. As the Archivist I have the papers of the period, and they would come forward with new ideas on what ought or ought not to be done, and they were solemnly put forward to the three Directors at the time, and they were equally solemnly crossed out, and everything went off as usual.'

There is, curiously enough, no published history of Heal's, which is another way of saying that a great deal of significant information about the firm, its philosophy, its products and its organisation will vanish with the death of the employees and members of the family who know about these things. It is a great pity.

Chapter Three   Eating out

'One must eat,' wrote Eileen Hooton-Smith in 1928, in her pleasant little book, *The Restaurants of London*, and went on:

'Nowadays people eat more and more in restaurants. The English took hardly to the habit; there were the great traditions of the English home and household hospitality. But London, at any rate, has taken to the restaurant life. People lunch in restaurants, dine in them, sup in them, dance and entertain in them. This is partly habit, partly modern day activity, and quite largely on account of the servant question.'

There have always been, of course, people and people. The people Mrs Hooton-Smith had more particularly in mind were the comfortably off, those who were affected by 'the servant question', perhaps five per cent of the population, at a generous estimate, in 1928. For the remainder of the British there were eating places of a different kind, 'those which provide meals at popular prices, and so on to the tea shop and fried fish type.' 'Popular prices', however, would not have meant the same thing to everyone.

'The price of lunch in Soho ranges from one and sixpence to four shillings; dinner from half-a-crown to five shillings; supper from half-a-crown to four shillings. A surprising number of courses are provided for the price.' This was undoubtedly excellent value, even in 1928, but this was a time when most manual workers earned between two and three pounds a week and the average teacher and civil servant could count on a maximum salary of no more than £500 a year. With all the other bills to pay, there was little margin for Soho lunches, or for their equivalent in other parts of the country. For the great bulk of English people in pre-Second World War days, there had to be a clear distinction between eating which had to be achieved regularly, and eating out, which was something for very special occasions.

In these circumstances, an eating-place could be successful on one of three levels, which one might briefly describe as Ritz level, Lyons Corner House level, and shop-house level. Cafés and pubs were a different matter. Mrs Hurst and her husband operated at chop-house level. In March 1915 they took over the Harp Dining Rooms in Maida Vale, London. They continued to run the restaurant until early in the 1939–45 War, when bombs put an end to the business.

As the photograph shows, what the Hursts had was a small double-fronted shop, with living accommodation above it. There were hundreds of similar establishments. They took the business over as a going concern from an elderly couple who had allowed it to sink to a very run-down condition. The premises were old and the takings were low. A great deal of hard work and enterprise was needed to bring the restaurant up to a reasonable standard again and to make it pay.

'We could seat about sixty people at a time,' Mrs Hurst recalled. 'Our customers were all kinds, because we provided them with good home cooking. I remember actors and actresses from the Kilburn Empire, Carmen, chauffeurs and removal men. We were open from Monday to Friday from seven in the morning to half-past six in the evening and on Saturdays from seven to half-past one.'

The Harp Dining Rooms, in other words, catered mainly for people who had to eat away from home during their working day. This meant sometimes breakfast, sometimes a midday meal. It did not include anything that could be described as pleasure eating, leisure eating or entertainment eating. It was not a place for the evenings or the weekend.

Mrs Hurst was really the key figure. 'We had one waitress in the shop and I looked after the cooking. There was a large coal-fired stove, with two very big ovens. The steamers were heated by gas. Another kitchen was used for making puddings and pastries and a third one for preparing vegetables and for washing up.

'All the food was fresh and the quality was good. We used to serve beef, lamb, liver and bacon, stewed steak, and then, to follow, apple pudding, raisin pudding, college pudding and plain suet pudding, with jam or marmalade or syrup.'

The furniture was solid and basic. 'There were some tables and chairs at the top of the shop and high-back wooden seats, taking about four people each. Some of our customers sat on stools. We had a counter for the tea and coffee urns.'

The Hursts looked after the Harp Dining Rooms for twenty-six years. They concentrated on what they understood, good materials and plain cooking, and they made a reasonable living. 'We were,' Mrs Hurst said with understandable pride, 'able to have a car and to go out to socials.' Apart from the bomb, they had no real complaints.

Distinctly down-market from the Harp Dining Rooms was

Mr and Mrs Hurst outside the Harp Dining Rooms, Maida Vale, early Twenties.

the East End tea-bar where Mrs Joyce Calder worked, completely illegally, in 1933–34, when she was ten years old. It was stationed during its working hours, that is, in the evenings, opposite the 'Boleyn Tavern', the nearest public house to West Ham football ground, and consequently very well known in the district, and it was garaged in the daytime in the Priory Mews Garage. The proprietor was a man whom Mrs Calder remembers as 'Jack'.

She helped out with serving. Jack paid her no wages, but her reward was something much closer to a child's heart, 'the pieces of pastry, coconut and icing left over in the trays and, of course, a lovely cheese cake now and again'.

There were no fixed hours for her. She was there whenever her father was working on his car nearby. 'He was a fanatic, and polished and cleaned it nearly every day when it wasn't in use.'

Later, in her teens, she got to know Jack's bar from another angle, 'after a visit to the local cinema or dance hall'. Her boy friends always paid for her, so she never paid much attention to the prices, but she remembers very well the fare that was on offer: 'Saveloys, meat pieces, Eccles cakes, cheese cakes, Camp coffee and tea'. She has fond memories of 'the hiss of powered paraffin lamps and the black and white oil-cloth on the counter'. The customers, as she remembers them, were a very varied lot, ranging from down-and-outs to well-to-do members of the middle-class. Subsequent investigation among some of her friends who also remember Jack's stall revealed that tea was 1d. a cup, cakes 1d. and 1½d., saveloys 1d. and Doubleday meat pies 2d., which could hardly be called expensive. The stall was economically run, especially in the matter of fuel. The saveloys and meat pies were kept warm on top of the tea urn.

Miss M. Laws went to work in the catering trade at just about the same time as Mrs Calder was pouring cups of tea for Jack.

49

Her working autobiography tells us a great deal about conditions at the time.

'I left school in 1932 to train as a commis waitress. I was paid 12 shillings a week, and out of that I had to pay 8 pence a day for a workman's ticket on the railway. If you missed the workmen's train, it cost you 1s. 10d. return, although, if you went on duty later, you could get a cheap day return for a shilling. The "2d. all the way" fares helped those who lived on the tram routes.

'In the catering trade, you were sure of three decent meals a day, which is why people took the job, with so many out of work. There was breakfast, lunch and tea, if you were on early turn, and supper instead of breakfast if you were on late duty. Experienced waitresses earned 16s. a week, minus 1s. a week for uniforms and 1s. 3d. for insurance stamps. The food was certainly worth more than the actual wage.'

Miss Laws worked for a large and unusually interesting restaurant chain, J.P. Restaurants. There were dozens of branches, mostly in the City and in the north and east of London. The concern had been started in Victorian times by John Pearce, with the aim of making it possible for working-class people to buy substantial, cheap meals. 'Pearce and Plenty' soon became a well-known slogan. Most of the shops went under the name of Pearce, but those in the better-class areas, where what was then known as 'the theatre trade' could be expected, were called J.P. Restaurants.

One of the last branches to be opened was in St Martin's Lane. Others were in Charing Cross Road, High Holborn, and Old Change, near St Paul's. The shop at Old Change was underground and the domed roof of the restaurant formed a small island in the roadway, which the traffic had to dodge. The business was taken over by the ABC in the mid-Thirties, and the names 'Pearce' and 'J.P.' were finally abolished at the end of the War.

Miss Laws was sent to the J.P. Restaurant in Shoe Lane for the first seven weeks. 'The manageress, Miss Bryant, spent her time telling me I wasn't a patch on my sister, who was seven years older than me and had worked there at one time. My work here consisted of cleaning silver-plated sugar-tongs, vegetable dishes, tea-pots and hot-water jugs, carrying dirty crockery to the 'wash-up' and changing tablecloths. The waitresses had to do all the cleaning of cutlery and cruets.

'At the end of seven weeks, I was promoted to the Victoria branch, at 29 Victoria Street. This saved me the daily walk from London Bridge Station to Shoe Lane, since my new shop was opposite Victoria Station. The huge ABC was on the opposite corner. When I arrived home with the news of my transfer, my sister said, "Oh, no hope for me," and left the firm. It was one

J.P. Restaurants in London during the 1930s

J.P. Restaurants catered for two fairly distinct types of trade. Broadly speaking, those in the E and EC postal districts did most of their business at lunchtime and the remaining branches were active in the middle of the day and in the evenings as well.

Both of the restaurants where Miss Laws worked, at St Martin's Lane and Victoria, came into the second category. The location-pattern of the thirty-eight restaurants is shown on the map, and the details are as follows:

Group A. Mainly lunches

4 Blomfield Street, EC2
3–4 Camomile Street, EC3
319 Central Market, EC1
8 City Road, EC1
17–18 Charterhouse Street, EC1
81 Charterhouse Street, EC1
Coventry House, South Place, EC2
49–50 Eastcheap, EC3
25 Eldon Street, EC2
39–40 Farringdon Road, EC1
49 Farringdon Road, EC1
1 Fenchurch Building, EC4
54 Finsbury Pavement, EC2
84 Fore Street, EC2
45 Golden Lane, EC1
31 Jewen Street, EC3
54–55 London Wall, EC2
2 Minories, EC3
1 New Basinghall Street, EC2
33 Newgate Street, E4
13A Old Change, EC4
5–6 Paternoster Row, EC4
2 and 2A St Andrew's Hill, EC4
35–36 Shoe Lane, EC4
73 Watling Street, SE18
36–38 Whitefriars Street, EC2

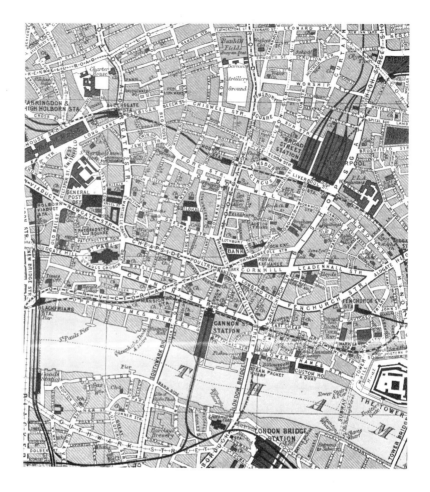

of their rules never to put relatives in the same shop, and she had been wanting to get there for years, because with the fast trade there was hope of getting many more tuppences left under the plates than in the quieter City shops, which really only filled up at lunch time.

'There were three shifts, 6 a.m. to 4 p.m. – you were allowed to go at 3.30, if you didn't want tea; 8 a.m. to 6 p.m.; and 11 a.m. to 9 p.m. Half an hour was allowed for breakfast, tea or supper and an hour for dinner. I worked from 8 to 6. The Young Persons' Act hadn't yet come into force, with the shorter hours if you were under 16. The Corner Girls, or washers-up, earned 17s. a week. I don't know how much Chef Warner earned, but he was a wonderful cook, with only a vegetable cook, by the name of George, to help him.

'Everything was freshly cooked each day. Roast beef, pie, toad-in-the-hole, lamb with mint sauce or redcurrant jelly, Lancashire hot-pot were all sold for around 1s. Boiled, mashed, roast or chipped potatoes were 3d. Most puddings – rice,

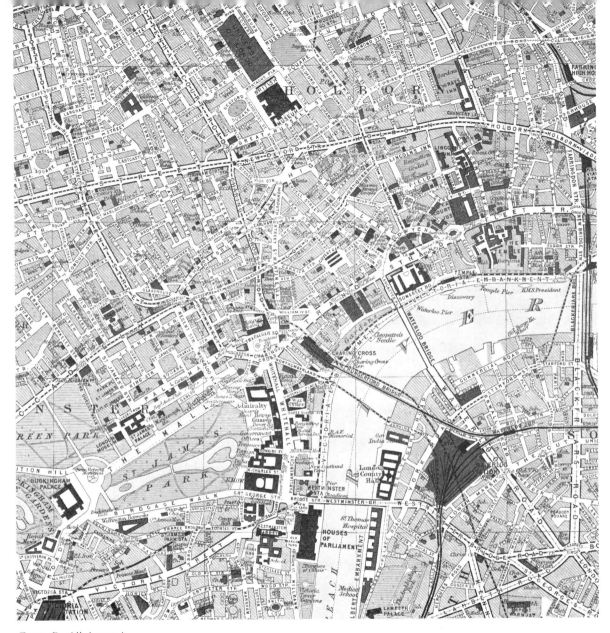

Group B. All-day trade

35 Carnaby Street, W1
152 Charing Cross Road, WC2
40 Drury Lane, WC2
18 Gray's Inn Road, WC1
266 High Holborn, WC1
79 New Oxford Street, WC1
359–361 Oxford Street, W1
142 Praed Street, W2
3–4 St Martin's Court, WC2
51 St Martin's Lane, WC2
165A Strand, WC2
3 Victorian Buildings, Victoria
   Station, SW1

cabinet, jam roll and so on – were 4d. A pot of tea was 3d., three small slices of bread and butter 2d., a roll and butter 2d. Fancy pastries made by W. H. Hill and Sons of Buckingham Gate were 2½d. each. Whole gorgeous Dundee cakes cost 3s. 3d. They were cut into 14 portions, at 3d. a portion. Devonshire teas at 9d. consisted of a pot of tea, two tiny buns, a scone and two little dishes, one containing an ice-cream scoop measure of real cream and the other raspberry jam.

'How Sally Roper or Lily Dowie, the grill maids (22s. a week) ever kept up with the trade beats me. All the grills took ten minutes. A steak or a chump or loin chop cost 1s., haddock

8d., eggs, fried, boiled or poached 3d., Scotch eggs 8d., sausages, tomatoes – they did the lot in the little box room beside the lift, which had to be hoisted aloft by pulling on the rope.

'The staff numbered about forty and we were all kept very busy, although, if there did happen to be an odd moment, we would try to persuade Grace Williams, one of a large talented family, to render 'Joscelin's Serenade', sitting on the staircase which led to the basement, with her arm through the balusters, plucking them as if they were an imaginary harp. She lived at Camberwell, and went to the same school as Elsie and Doris Waters, only they were in a higher class.

'The working conditions were good. There was no squalor. We kept the place scrubbed clean with bars of soap, 'Brookers's', and whiting, and Simoniz and soda. We didn't appreciate the rats, though. They lurked in many of the shops round about. At Victoria, we could look out of the window in the wash-up and see them gambolling between the rails of the Underground. The rat-catcher and his terrier kept the numbers down.

'The waitresses wore black dresses, made by the firm's own dressmaker, who worked in the Head Office in Charterhouse Street. They were made of serge, and they didn't often get a wash, as there were no spin driers in those days, and it was tricky to get a dress washed, dried and ironed on a Sunday, ready for wearing on a Monday. Black shoes, black stockings at 9d. a pair from Marks and Spencers – rayon, which laddered at the first snag. White caps, collars, cuffs and aprons, also laundered at home.

'The white cotton piqué overalls were changed twice a week, which meant fourteen buttons and rings had to be taken out and put in the clean overall. The overalls were laundered free of charge by the firm.

'In January 1937, I moved to Brighton and worked at the Regent for years, a vastly different place, now also pulled down – restaurant, silver service, Ship Café, cinema, ballroom to accommodate 2,000 dancers – oh, the lovely gowns, before the War came along to spoil everything.'

In the Twenties and Thirties the Regent was one of the biggest entertainment, eating and drinking complexes in Britain. Officially, the ballroom held 1,800 people, although during the Second World War there were times when as many as 2,200 were packed in. It was reckoned to have the finest spring floor in the country and the investment paid off. Every possible way of getting the people in was tried – big name bands, late night extensions, competition dancing, demonstrations and, every afternoon, the famous Regent tea dances.

'Gilt painted chairs and tables surrounded the floor. There

Staff at The Regent, Brighton, c. 1937. The photograph was taken in the main banqueting room, known as the Georgian Room. Those whose names Miss Laws can remember – a remarkable feat of memory – are:

Front row, sitting left to right: Mr Roberts, storekeeper; Mrs Harman, manageress; Percy Wheatland, chef; Mr Lamb; Mr Pasquali Amerina, catering manager who, in 1937, had been head waiter in the Restaurant; Mr Tannock; Mrs Roberts, manageress, wife of Mr Roberts, the storekeeper; and, at the end of the row, the cellarman, Peter Povey.

Centre row, the Ballroom waitresses – Lilian Peterson; Winnie Williams; Rose Kempson; then one whose name I can't remember; then Micky, the Polish waitress, sitting in full view –

her real name was Evelyn Sonia Kemp – an Irish girl, called Shannon; the half-hidden head of Lilian Bowyer; the eyes only of Dolly Goodyear; the cashiers just in front of the barmaids in the back row; I can't remember the name of the lass peeping round Mrs Harman's head; Mrs Young Eva, from Thornaby-on-Tees, who drove Flash, the horse on the milk cart during the War – when hair was needed for the mane and tail of a small wooden horse, while toys were scarce, Flash lost a bit of his tail; next, eyes only, behind the chef's hat, Rosemary Thomsett, the office girl.

I'm unsure of the names of the next three, all Ship Café staff; next Mrs Jackson, in white overall; Mrs Fern, the tea lady, just in front of my white overall; Mrs Violet Jones; I can't remember the little lady with specta-

cles; blonde Stella is next; just behind Mr Amerina is Mrs Law, who died in 1976 at the grand old age of 96; I forget the next counterhand and the beautiful blonde waitress seen between Mrs Amerina and Mr Tannock; Pat Seef, the dark-haired Irish waitress; Mary Brazier; I don't remember the little one behind Mrs Roberts; Rosie Smith, the waitress; 'Chris', Mrs Christmas; Audrey Hewitt, the waitress, now about 80; the last waitress, next to Peter the cellarman, is Ivy Ridgeon.

Back row, the eight barmaids of the Tudor Bar. Number 4 is Eileen Cahill and Number 5 Kathleen. I am at centre back, then come two cooks; Pamela Thrush, whose father had been Control Clerk in 1937; the remainder of the people in this row are cleaners.

were about three hundred of them, spread with yellow damask cloths, although during the War, when the troops were enjoying their pints, it was found more economical, from the point of laundry bills, to have green checked tablecloths.

'Even with the poor wages of the 1920s and 1930s, the wage bill must have been colossal – page boys, lift attendants, potmen, silver cleaners, washers up, cooks and other kitchen staff, plumbers, electricians, projectionists, usherettes, kiosk sales staff, office staff, cleaners. We even had our own bakery, making everything from bread to petit fours.

'When I applied for my job there, I was new to the town and I was shocked to see four long queues stretching from the Labour Exchange, past the Curzon Cinema next door. I was offered two jobs, a counterhand at Bertrams at 18s. a week – that meant working at Brighton Station buffet – or a counterhand at the Regent, £1. Naturally, I took the second one. Food was provided, and it was only a 1d. tram ride to get to work. "Could I make a pot of tea and toast?" asked Mr "Nello" Fabrina, who was always addressed as Mr Nello. "Yes," I said, and I was in.'

The archaeology of restaurants and cafés is a sadly neglected field of research. More than any other type of commercial premises, they have been obliterated, concealed or transformed by mergers, bankruptcies and closures. A high proportion of pre-1939 catering businesses proved to be too small for survival in a world which demanded new kinds of service and amenity. Many were in streets and blocks which have been pulled down for development, many others were annihilated by bombing. Very few are recorded in photographs and even fewer are documented by the survival of menus or business papers. The social historian in search of source material has particularly difficult problems with the catering industry and it is for this reason especially that personal reminiscences are so important.

What is certain, however, is that catering workers have always been a remarkably mixed body of people. With the long hours and often very tiring and disagreeable working conditions, this is usually a trade that one drifts into from necessity, rather than enters from choice.

With jobs of all kinds so hard to find and hold in the Twenties and Thirties, and without the cushion of the modern Welfare State, one might reasonably suppose that the level of person employed in hotels and restaurants at that time would have been rather higher than has been the case in recent years. Evidence either to support or disprove this view is not easy to find, but it certainly seems probable that boys and girls who had left school at fourteen found it easier to achieve posts of responsibility during that period, when educational opportunities were far fewer, when experience, especially good experience, was greatly valued, and when it was more normal that it is today to owe one's success to enterprise, intelligence and, of course, luck.

For those in the top catering posts, excellent salaries were available – in 1930 the chef at a big London hotel could reckon to earn without too much difficulty £1,000 a year, which was a great deal of money in those days – but the way to such heights was very hard. An apprentice chef would be paid no more than 7s. 6d. a week to begin with, together with his food, and he would frequently have to work twelve hours a day. Apprenticeships were extremely difficult to get and, at the most prestigious establishments, such as the Ritz or the Savoy, considerable influence was required before one was even granted an interview.

Once he was accepted, a fourteen-year-old apprentice would find himself thrown straight from school into the noisy and far from gentle world of a hotel kitchen, without the slightest preparation or training. If he happened to be working for a major concern, especially in London, he would almost certainly have to come to terms with French from the start. The people around him might or might not be French – most of the apprentices came from somewhere in the British Isles and many of the pastrycooks were German or Swiss – but French, or rather, kitchen French, was the lingua franca of the trade, and one had to learn to understand it and use it pretty quickly or get out. But, in a good place, there were compensations – much better meals than one would have eaten at home and half a bottle of wine a day which, for a boy in his mid-teens, amounted to very luxurious living indeed. And in his second year he would be earning about 12s. 6d., which compared well with what he would have been getting in other occupations.

There was competition for people who had been trained as waiters or cooks in the best hotels and restaurants, and there was a great deal of voluntary movement from one job to another, sometimes for the sake of better money or a more reasonable employer, but just as often simply for a change or in order to widen one's experience. The slower pace of a club might seem attractive after the bustle and constant high pressure of a big hotel; a spell of waiting might be fitted in between two kitchen jobs; Torquay, Harrogate or Edinburgh would give one a chance to see more of the country. And restaurant staff, very understandably, can get tired of dealing with the same kind of people day after day. After a few years in the staid atmosphere of the Reform Club or the Athenaeum, a place frequented by the literary or theatrical world could have its charm. And there were always brand-new restaurants entering the field, where one could enjoy the stimulus of a new style of

The Ritz dining room, Piccadilly, in the early Seventies: decor has changed little since the Thirties.

décor and catering, a management committed to making the venture succeed and, if one was lucky, the opportunity to rise and prosper with the establishment. For someone who was tired of getting home every day at midnight, a lunchtime-only restaurant could be very enticing, especially if one were getting on in years. Some of the big London stores offered this kind of opportunity and got very good staff as a result. In a restaurant like the famous Rainbow Room at Derry and Toms in Kensington, work was hectic during the middle part of the day, but one had the comfort of knowing that when the store closed, the restaurant closed too, and that meant not only free evenings, but free Sundays as well.

For casual and unskilled workers in the industry, conditions could be very bad, with low wages, harsh discipline and insecurity built into the job, but for someone who had had a proper hotel or restaurant training and who was prepared to move around in search of opportunities, the Great Depression was tolerable. 'I have never been out of work', one of these fortunate breed told us when he was in his mid-seventies. 'God has been very good to me.'

The Rainbow Room, Derry and Toms, mid-Thirties. The name was apt. 'Over the restaurant is a tiered ceiling of light slots, of curvatures that give even brightness over the whole area. The use of coloured neon tubes in these slots further contributes to the evenness of lighting. The ceiling seems to float overhead as though one were inside a balloon, an effect which cannot be presented properly in a photograph. The value of evenness of lighting is clearly demonstrated. Red, green and blue tubes in each slot allow a pleasant diversity of colourings to be rendered.' (The Architect and Building News, 14 April 1933)

Not all hotel and restaurant staff have been as lucky or as much in love with life. Without any doubt, few people today would be willing to work as hard as waitresses and kitchen staff before 1939 did, or for so little money.

Mrs L. Brown, as she now is, worked for J. Lyons in the Thirties. She trained at the restaurant attached to the Strand Palace Hotel, built, like its sister hotel, the Regent Palace, just before the 1914–18 War. They formed part of what a contemporary observer called 'that huge and wonderfully organised mechanism for eating which Messrs J. Lyons and Co. have spread over London'. The Corner House Restaurants, as they were known, were planned and fitted out to make people with very little money feel as if they had a great deal more. There was plenty of marble and mirrors, lounges with basket chairs, orchestras, chandeliers and a general atmosphere of grandeur and luxury. Until, in the 1950s, popular taste swung round to smaller, more intimate and more casual establishments, the Corner Houses were extremely successful. They did for eating out exactly what Burtons did for men's clothes – gave people with modest incomes the opportunity to indulge in something which had the taste of the pleasures of the rich about it.

Making you feel good in the Twenties and Thirties – the architecture of the Strand Palace Hotel lives up to its name.

Lyons achieved the miracle by means of superb organisation and by the sheer scale of the enterprise. In no other way could excellent lunches have been provided for 2s. 3d. and excellent dinners for 3s. 6d., especially in such surroundings. But the staff were tightly disciplined and driven very hard. This was part of the organisation, the part that was not shown to the public. Mrs Brown stuck it out for four years and then moved on to something a little less tough.

'The pay,' she well remembers, 'was 27s. 6d. a week, but we had "discrepancies" stopped from that, which very often left me owing J. Lyons money. For instance, if we forgot to charge customers for rolls and butter, or if someone stole them, which they often did, or if we forgot to enter some item on the customer's bill, we had to pay for this ourselves. So we relied on tips. I suppose on a good day we could make £1 this way,

59

60

The Strand Palace Hotel, part of the restaurant.

which was good in those days.

'Hours were long, with hardly any chance to rest, just a half-hour tea or supper break, while someone else took over our station, as our group of tables was called. We relieved them in turn. We had a very strict manager, Mr Kerry.

'The "Old English Waitresses" were the salt of the earth and most pleasant and reliable at all times. But things changed. I remember the refugees coming in, and what a mixed crowd they were – Germans, Austrians, Poles, even one from Estonia. Later, we had soldiers invalided out from the Army. They thought the Corner House discipline was worse than the Army.

'I remember one refugee who was carrying her tray poised like an open umbrella. It was full of cold, half-empty tea-pots and milk jugs. She dropped the lot and a hinged-lid teapot landed on a man's bald head. I shall never forget the sight of her wiping the tea-leaves off the poor man's head with her stained end-of-the-day serviette.

Strand Corner House as it was in the Sixties.

61

'After I left Lyons, I worked in a Greek restaurant in Charing Cross Road, then at Bearmans in Leytonstone, and then at a friend's market café. After that I opened a café in Cornwall with my husband.'

Everything seems different from the inside. Mrs Rene Chatfield found the Lyons Tea Shop in Paris Street, Woolwich, a wonderfully romantic place when she was in her teens. She and her friends used to go there after Church Parade at the Garrison Church.

'What a great occasion it was, with "Nippy" (Lyons' own special name for their waitresses) taking your order for a cup of tea – a real china cup *and* saucer – a separate dish for lumps of sugar, and the waitress writing the order down on the pad attached to her waist on a long piece of cord. There was no shouting orders down hatches, as there was in other places, or over the counter, and the lovely fresh hot cups of tea came from tea-pots, not urns.

'On one occasion I remember a woman coming into the shop carrying a dog. She was served by Nippy and then the woman took her saucer, put it on the floor and filled it with tea for the dog to drink, which it did. Nippy then calmly walked across, without saying a word, picked up the saucer and broke it in half on the table, and walked away, still without saying anything.'

The mark of a real professional. One wonders how the same incident would have been dealt with nowadays. But it is the kind of significant story which is most unlikely to figure in any official history of J. Lyons and Co.

No attempt has been made to preserve either a Lyons Corner House or a Lyons Teashop as the important social monuments they undoubtedly were. A museum of catering is long overdue and, to make proper sense, it would have to be in an old restaurant, where the environment would be part of the story. It could even be profitable and attractive to serve yesterday's meals in yesterday's way, on a regular basis, and one day maybe this will be done. There are a few restaurants, of course, like Simpsons in the Strand, where the old tradition has never been broken, and where we can continue to eat much as our fathers and grandfathers did, in a room where the furniture, layout and style remain more or less intact. But such places are increasingly rare. Catering archaeology, as we have already pointed out, is frustratingly thin on the ground.

But memories, both from staff and from customers, are fortunately in abundant supply, once one sets out to look for them. Seaside towns, where the catering industry has always been of special importance, can provide a rich crop. Mrs M. Aldrick, for instance, remembers the Bournemouth are very well.

'I came to Hampshire from Surrey, having been educated at a

Grammar School, but not reaching Matric standard. I applied for a job at a dairy shop in New Milton, but they needed a girl who had passed Matriculation to serve in their shop. This was in 1931. My uncle was manager of Voysey's of Boscombe, with five or six bakery and confectionery shops with cafés to control, as well as the main bakery. My first job was an apprenticeship with this firm.

'It was nearly a year before I was allowed to serve in the cake shop. My duties consisted of sweeping and cleaning the shop, washing up, and preparing teas. The errand boy did the scrubbing, both outside and inside the shop. The shop was at Cross Roads, Southbourne, and the café was quite a large one, with a busy summer trade. Afternoon tea was very popular in those days and I remember a good class customer used the café, both for morning coffee and afternoon tea. Light lunches were provided, too, and the three girls, the errand boy and the manageress were kept very busy. We also served teas at the bowling green, a short distance away. I felt very promoted when I was allowed to do this on my own after two years.

'The coffee was made in large enamel jugs. Boiling water was poured on the ground coffee, the grounds were allowed to settle, and it was then strained. Only pots of tea were served, no cups. Lunches were cottage pie with vegetables, ham with salads, sausages with mashed potatoes, and so on. Voysey's cakes were renowned and this accounted for the popularity of the café.

'I worked there for five years, after my three years' apprenticeship period. I moved to first sales girl at the firm's more important shops. For some of the time I cycled to work each day, leaving home about 7 o'clock each morning with my father, who worked at a large grocer's in Bournemouth. It seems strange to me to think that these occupations are rather looked down on now. At the time we felt they were rather high class. I felt I was very privileged to work at this cake shop and café when I was in my teens.

'I started work at 8 a.m. and finished at 7 p.m., but on Fridays it was 8 p.m. and on Saturdays at 9. I then had to cycle the 11 miles home, via Christchurch and the lanes to Bransgore. When we moved to New Milton, it was 13 miles to cycle each way. When I started, my wages were 5s. a week, with a rise of 2s. 6d. each year. Usually, food not used one day was made into cottage pie or meat pies the next. The staff were given this for their meals.

'I think cleanliness was much better in the 1930s. The corners of the room were scrubbed and the lino polished thoroughly at least once a week and the tables were always moved to allow this to be done. A few days ago at a restaurant I went into in Bristol there were no clean knives among the dozens in the tray.

When I pointed this out to the assistant and asked for a clean knife, she said it was the fault of the washing-up machine. The knives were not only spotted, but they had food sticking to them.'

It is never easy to decide how to interpret comments of this kind, simply because one does not know how typical the café in Bournemouth and the restaurant in Bristol were. What is certain however, is that in 1931 restaurant staff were cheap and easy to get and that in 1978, when Mrs Aldrick had her nasty experience with the knives, they were relatively expensive, hard to recruit and tended to leave forthwith if discipline showed signs of becoming tough. Before 1939, the restaurant trade could reckon on always having an adequate supply of skilled, experienced people to do the work; nowadays the business is organised on the assumption that one will have to employ whom one can, and that the less skill that is demanded, the more smoothly and profitably the restaurant is likely to run. In the Thirties, if knives were dirty, one simply dismissed the person who had failed to clean them properly; nowadays one waits more or less patiently for the mechanic to arrive to put the machine right, while the assistant – the only person with whom the public comes into contact – self-righteously disclaims all responsibility. The restaurants and cafés which have been unable or unwilling to come to terms with the new order have simply faded out of the picture, unless they were in a position to charge prices high enough to allow the traditional system and methods to be artificially preserved and to run what was in effect a culinary museum.

Mr Henri Travers, of St Peter Port, Guernsey, saw clearly what was happening to the catering trade after the Second World War and decided to call it a day. The restaurant at the Prince of Wales no longer exists and Mr Travers has a much quieter and probably just as prosperous a life running the place as an ordinary pub. This is the story as he told it.

'My great-grandfather came over here from Dorset to assist with the building of the harbour. He put his son, James J. Travers, to an apprenticeship with a printer, and this man, my grandfather, started the business here at the Prince of Wales in 1884. Here, in the present bar, is the original licence. It's in French and it's dated 3 September 1884, and signed "Greffier de la Reine". At the top it says, "Acte d'Autorisation", and it's made out to "Monsieur James Travers", giving him the right to "exercer le métier de cabaretier dans une maison située à la rue des Forges".

'At the front of the stairs, there's a certificate from the Guernsey Licensed Victuallers Protection Association. It says: "This Testimonial has been presented to James J. Travers, together with a gold watch-chain and a silver tea-pot for Mrs

The 'Prince of Wales' in 1897.

The 'Prince of Wales', Guernsey, decked out for the Coronation of Edward VII, 1902.

65

Travers, by the above Association as a mark of esteem for valuable services rendered by him as Honorary Secretary and Treasurer''. And then there's the names of the committee, the date, 1899, and a portrait of my grandfather.

'His wife was French. The bar was downstairs. The dear old lady was rather good at cooking, so in the bar she started to cook for the customers and she did very well. Her kitchen in the basement was the place now labelled ''Gents''. It was a sort of coaching inn and the stables were next door. My grandfather took over the stables and gradually extended and eventually opened up the restaurant upstairs on the ground floor. You can still see ''Restaurant'' etched on the windows and we've got cups with grandfather's initials on them. The kitchen for the new ground-floor restaurant was where the ''Ladies Only'' is now. And eventually we had a restaurant upstairs as well.

'We only ran a lunch. It was a lunch place, with special meals in the evenings. The customers were business people in the town, accountants, lawyers, people like that. And we used to do quite a lot with the school, the college. Parents used to bring their youngsters to have a meal here. We charged two shillings before the War and 2s. 6d. just after it. It was a three course

The present street-level bar at the 'Prince of Wales', formerly the dining-room.

The 'Prince of Wales' as it is today.

meal, with the meat carved off the joint.

'When the motor-car came in after the 1914 War, the restaurant trade went down, because people could go home to lunch easily. The summer visitors didn't make all that difference to us. We had an all-the-year-round trade. But there wasn't a lot of competition. In the old days there were only two other restaurants in the town. None of them were big restaurants. We could seat about twenty people.

'We gradually built the business up during the Twenties and Thirties and then the war changed everything. The States – the Essential Commodities – took over the restaurant and used it as a kind of canteen for their staff. They put someone in to run it. They used to bring their own stuff in, whatever they could get. Just like any other café or restaurant in town during the Occupation. I gave a bit of help. Of course, the bars had to close down. There was nothing to sell.

'We carried on for about ten years after the war and then we closed the restaurant down. We use the upstairs restaurant and kitchen as part of our own accommodation now. Towards the end, the trade had slackened off a good deal. We were really running the restaurant more or less for the sake of tradition then. We weren't making much profit out of it.'

And there it is, a pleasant pub with a great deal of a museum about it. Apart from the innumerable pictures on the walls, there's a nice collection of pistols and powder flasks, with the official German receipt when they were handed in for safe keeping in April 1941. Another relic of the Occupation is a ship's bell. 'That came off a French tanker, the "Tolcan", that used to run in here with oil for the Germans. When the

Normandy landings took place, we were cut off, of course. The French crew were very short of grub and they flogged the ship's bell to someone in the country for food. Luckily enough, the farmer was a customer of mine, and after the War he was short of Scotch. I had some, and we bartered the bell for that.'

The people who ate regularly at the Prince of Wales regarded themselves as a kind of club and they were in the habit of sending telegrams to the Prince of Wales (the future Edward VII) himself from time to time. The Prince's Private Secretary always wired back and there are several of these replies, framed, on the walls. One, sent from Sandringham, says:

'Mr Travers, Prince of Wales Hotel, Guernsey. The Prince of Wales thanks the diners at your hotel for your kind congratulations and in the unfortunate event of war is sure Guernsey will do its duty. Knollys.'

It is a little difficult to imagine a similar exchange of telegrams between Royalty and the people taking a light lunch at Voysey's Café in Bournemouth or eating out at the Strand Palace, but the patrons of an old-style place like the Hursts' Harp Dining Rooms might just conceivably have done so.

The on-site archaeology of eating becomes steadily rarer, and the Prince of Wales is a refreshing exception. How many other restaurants or ex-restaurants can boast, for example, a 1902 cash register? Mr Travers still has one, with the original guarantee still stuck to the bottom. 'When decimalisation came in,' he recalls, 'we had it modified, but it's a bit of a nuisance, really, because it only tells up to about 40p.'

Chapter Four   Three glovers

It is a curious fact that gloves have had only one historian in Britain, S. William Beck, who carried out his researches in the late Victorian period, at a time when the wearing of gloves was universal among both men and women with the slightest pretensions to gentility and when the trade boomed as a result. Those were the days when there were no imports from the Far East to undercut the market and bring British and French manufacturers to despair and bankruptcy. They were also the days of abundant cheap labour, when the sewing of gloves was carried out largely by women and girls in their own homes, for disgracefully little money. The story of gloves has some unpleasant aspects to it.

By the second half of the nineteenth century, the pattern of the industry was well established. The three leading firms, Dents, Fownes and Allcrofts all had their warehouse and head office in London, their factories in the provinces and their very respectable and well-paid travellers – the kings of commercial representatives – covering the country. Certain areas, Worcestershire, Wiltshire and Somerset, were pre-eminent on the manufacturing side, but throughout the nineteenth and twentieth centuries the business was carried on quite widely over the Southern and Western counties. The method of organisation was basically similar everywhere. There was a factory where the skins were stored and the gloves cut, and a large number of women in the villages and small towns within an area of five or ten miles around the factory who stitched the gloves. Each week, occasionally more often, someone from the factory called at the women's houses to bring cut gloves for sewing and to take away the finished work. The gloving firms still rely heavily on outworkers today, although nowadays the work moves to and from the factory by van, not as formerly by pony and trap. Where the outworkers lived close to the factory, they usually picked up the gloves themselves from the factory and took the work back again afterwards.

During the eighteenth century, the heavy import duty on foreign gloves made them an important part of the British smuggling trade. When this was repealed in 1825, the English manufacturers largely gave up competing with the French for the high fashion market, preferring to concentrate on the heavier gloves, especially for men, and to import high fashion women's gloves from the principal French firms.

With the serious contraction of the market for leather gloves during the present century, there have been many mergers and takeovers, with the result that the Dent, Fownes, Allcroft triumvirate no longer exists as separate companies. First came a joint company, Dent Fownes and now there is only Dent Allcroft. The present Dent Allcroft concern is the product of many takeovers and shut-downs over the past fifty years.

What might be called the archaeology of the gloving industry consequently falls into three parts – the factories, the central warehouses and office buildings and, much more numerous, the cottages where the sewing was carried out. The first two of these have suffered great casualties, not least during the Second World War, when air-raids on London did great damage to premises of both Fownes and Dent and, saddest of all, destroyed nearly all their business records.

Mr G. J. Carmen (this is a pseudonym) began work in 1936 at Fownes in London.

'I joined the warehouse after going in circles to find a job at the end of the Depression period, when you were very pleased to get any sort of job. I was taken on as a boy. You started in the postal section, despatch section. There used to be an old martinet there, a fellow called Dick Atkins. When you'd been there some while, you'd be promoted to entering up the daily orders, which would come in by post. The post was pretty big in those days, of course. The warehouse was in Gresham Street, right next to the Guildhall. In fact the Guildhall has now taken over the property. It caught fire. They had a fire bomb, it was right next door to the Old Jewry Church, it used to tie up with the Guildhall a lot. Dents were about two hundred yards away in Wood Street, 97 Wood Street.

'Living in was quite normal in those days. The top floor of the building was just dormitories, you see. You'd sleep there. There'd be a housekeeper and maids for making up beds. We always employed men and boys. In fact the City of London had hardly any women at all working in it in those days, apart from a few typists or stenographers. If you went out into the City of London – the Textile Square as they called it, Cheapside – you'd hardly ever see a girl or woman in 1935 or 1936.'

For an office boy, to get into gloving was to join the City's élite.

'I started off very well. I started at £1 a week, which was a very good wage, but when I look back on it, it used to cost me 10d. a day to go up by train – that was by workman's – to get to London by eight o'clock. I sometimes missed the train. Like all kids, I used to sleep a bit late. When I did that, it cost me 1s. 10d., and that was six days a week. If you took the workman's, it was 10d., which made five bob out from your £1 a week wages.

'We used to take our own lunch. We used to sit in the boiler room to eat that. There used to be a man around the boiler room and he used to keep us boys sitting on wooden cases there, well under control, and of course, when I became wealthy and got half a crown rise, on pay days we used to go out, half a dozen boys, buy ourselves a lunch. It used to cost us 10d. for a three-course lunch, waitress served, and it would be a real treat, soup, steak and kidney pie, and a sweet afterwards, and if you were very rich, you used to leave ½d. or 1d., as a tip.'

Working there in the London warehouse, the young apprentice saw practically nothing of the real business of glove-making. Occasionally, though, there were outings to the factory in Worcester, where the London people were able to see different kinds of gloves being made.

The warehouse was the power centre of the business. This was the distribution centre, the place where the English and the imported gloves were brought together and where the current ranges were prepared. It was also the base from which the firm's travellers operated. Mr Carmen remembers one of them, called Bell, who used to come in regularly for a chat long after he had retired and talk about the conditions a traveller worked under in the old days.

'He'd been a traveller up to the Yorkshire area. He used to go up by train and then go out to the Dales on horseback, a man with a packhorse behind him carrying his samples. They were welcomed in like Royalty. They laid their samples out, took the order, probably in March or April for the following delivery, in August, September, when the winter was coming on. At the same time, they used to collect the cash for the previous year, in gold sovereigns, which used to be sent down to London in leather purses made specially for the purpose.

'They were extremely wealthy people, the travellers, and the buyers and managers in the gloving business. There was another old fellow, Robert Side. I lived in the same house as he did in south-east London, a house he lived in when he got married. At that time, he was earning somewhere about £700–£800 a year, which was a lot of money in those days.'

Some of the travellers went on using horse transport until the 1920s.

'Motor cars came out between the wars. Travellers then used to have to buy their own cars. They were advanced cash by the company and then had to repay it, over a period. But even up to 1939 the London traveller used to go round the West End in the horse and brougham, as it was then, and deliveries used to be made by horse and cart – the town cart as they called it. And everything was such a rush. An order would be done in the morning and he would have to go out on the two o'clock cart, to deliver it the same day. The warehouse was geared up to do it.'

Until the Second World War put an end to so many of the niceties of life, gloving, for the travellers and management, was an exceedingly gentlemanly affair, totally untouched by the American way of doing business. When a new traveller was appointed, Fownes announced the change to the customers in these terms:

'March, 1927.

Dear Sir(s),

We feel sure that you will share our regret at having to announce to you that our Mr H. J. Jones, who has so ably represented us in Ireland for so many years, has decided, owing to ill-health, to retire on a pension.

We have pleasure in advising you that we have appointed as his successor Mr S. W. Meyer, of 4 Castle Market, Dublin, who has been in Ireland for many years and is thoroughly acquainted with the glove trade, and is, no doubt, well-known to you.

We trust that the friendly relations which have always existed between us will suffer no interruption from this change.

We remain, Dear Sirs,

Yours faithfully,

Fownes Brothers & Co.'

Mr Carmen stayed at the warehouse until the Second World War temporarily removed him from circulation. When he came back, at the age of 27, he was soon made a buyer, 'one of the youngest buyers ever made', and it immediately became clear to him that the old days had gone for ever. Gloving was in for a hard time.

'The majority of the labour had gone over to war work, light engineering and so on, which was obviously much better paid. This coincided with the period when foreign imports, particularly from the Far East, started to develop and the industry had no protection whatsoever. It declined not only in this country but in the whole of Europe – the French industry, the Belgian industry, the German industry all vanished. There is still a nucleus left of the British industry, which concentrates on better quality. We hope we have got a measure of protection coming through the Common Market. The industry has gone too far, really, to recover. The potential demand is smaller.'

The future is a matter for speculation, but what has happened summarised and symbolised by a complex of efficient modern buildings at Warminster in Wiltshire, where Mr Carmen now finds himself working. It is a logical place for what may well be one of the industry's last bastions. The Warminster–Wiltshire area contained three major gloving firms in the Thirties: J. and T. Beavan; Boulton Bros., and A. L. Jefferies Ltd. Beavan's still continues as an independent concern, but the other two, like Fownes, were absorbed by Dent, Allcroft and Co.

The result of this is that one can meet at the Warminster headquarters of Dent Fownes a number of people who have spent much of their working life with other companies. One of them is Mr R. D. Jefferies, whose family business, A. L. Jefferies Ltd, was established in Fore Street, Westbury, in 1883. It had a modern factory in Warminster as well, the present Dent Fownes premises, and it sold out to Dent Allcroft in 1938. Jefferies' Westbury factory was in what had once been a group of cottages.

Mr Jefferies went into the business straight from school.

'I was fourteen. I started numbering, pairing numbers on racks. Went on to do a bit of cutting and made a few gloves along the line. Leather sorting as well. We had a leather finishing section at Midsomer Norton in those days. I had eighteen months there, finishing chiefly shammy in those days.

'We were using outworkers very considerably then. At one time I used to go over to Melksham to a house there to inspect hand-sewn making around the Melksham district. This was in 1936 and I travelled by car, an Austin 10. I learned to drive it in 1933.'

When war broke out in 1939, he was earning £2 10s. a week. His Army pay compared favourably with his civilian earnings.

'I was in the Royal Wiltshire Yeomanry, I was called up and had six years abroad. Then I came back. The Westbury premises were still being used and I was there sorting leather for cutting for eighteen months. After that I came up here in Warminster into the warehouse. Then I went to Southampton – we had a place at Southampton then – and I was there for four years. Southampton closed, and I came back here again, again in the warehouse on the fabric side, and eventually got back into the factory. There was a period of four years, I suppose, when I was designing.'

Mr Jefferies now runs the manufacturing side at Warminster, where one of his most experienced colleagues is Fred Ridout, who began work with the Jefferies' company in Westbury fifty-three years ago, when he was fourteen.

'I went to do cutting out button-holes and things like that, pasting leather together. It was all leather in those days. I was paid 4s. 6d. a week. We used to start at half past seven and work till six. There was quite a few people working at Westbury

The cutting room at Westbury in the Twenties.

then. I expect there was fifty easy. There was a lot of girls, too, upstairs, in what we used to call "the business", where Mr Willy, Mr Jefferies' grandfather, used to be.'

When he was sixteen, Mr Ridout started to learn a skilled trade, as a cutter. Conditions in the cutting room could hardly be described as luxurious.

'In cutting you don't need any heating, you know, because you've got the physical movement all the time. We had those old Tortoise stoves, do you remember those? Mr James was our foreman. He always used to put a tin of water on there to damp the air, it boiled and steam came off, just like they put on the front of the radiators, a humidifier. You had one of these stoves at each end of the room. It was a big room. They were big stoves. It wasn't too bad.

'In those days we didn't have canteen facilities. We had a room opposite – an old cottage. We used to go over there midday. Somebody used to light the stove and we'd go over there and have our dinner. And then we'd go down the field and have a game of football.'

74

The apprenticeship to cutting was a short one, only two years, and after a few years at this, Mr Ridout went on to another job.

'Five or six years before the War I finished cutting. Then I went on sorting leather and putting up the cutting for the cutters. It was still at Westbury, but in a different place, round the Post Office, Westbury House. Cutting was a skilled job, but sorting was an advance for me.'

In gloving, as in tailoring, much of the profit is made or lost in the way the skins or the cloth are cut. With the soft leathers, the skill lies in seeing where the blemishes are and in avoiding them when the skin is laid out for cutting and, at the same time, in planning the cutting so that one finishes up with the minimum amount of waste and in stretching it before cutting.

'The difference between shoe-cutting and glove-cutting is that in shoe-cutting the leather's firm, there's no movement in it, you've got to pull it about to make sure the glove fits. If you don't have just the right amount of leather, then the glove either folds up or goes out of shape. You don't have no fit.'

So a gloving firm is indeed very dependent on its leather sorters and cutters for success, and has always paid them well. In the Thirties, as the photograph shows, there were plenty of young men willing to take up the trade, but since then the skilled labour force has got steadily older. It has been a serious source of worry for the gloving firms, especially since the work cannot be mechanised.

But Mr Ridout was one of the men who came back to the business after the war. He picked up his old trades of cutting and sorting, moving from one of the firm's centres to another, to Westbury, to Midsomer Norton, to Radstock – 'we had a hut, stayed there for quite a time until Mr Brown retired'.

The leather at that time came mainly from their own tannery at Hawkridge, not far from Westbury, where they dealt with parcels of imported skins. Some of these were known as EIs – EI standing for East India.

'They were graded by unit size. EIs were bought in great big bales, and they used to be sorted by weight. The thin ones went to women's gloves, the heavy ones went to men's. It was an old factory there at Hawkridge, and they had those big tumblers, you know, for washing and soaking the skins on the ground floor and then the skins were gradually moved up the floors. I think the sorting room was out the back. After we gave up the tannery, the building was used at one time for one of those battery fowl places. Some furriers had it at one time, too.'

That was the time when every glove factory of any size used to dress their own skins. Nowadays, soft leather dressing is carried on almost entirely by two firms, one at Yeovil, the other at Abingdon, both operating on a very large scale. And nearly all the skins used today come from Africa, especially from Ethiopia, where the sheep and goats live hard. Well-fed animals produce skins that are too thick and coarse for making good quality gloves.

After the war, Fred Ridout took work round to the outworkers, having learnt to drive when he was in the Army. In his opinion, the women were making a reasonable living.

'I thought they were in those days, yes. It was all according to speed and skill. It was a better job than up in London. Did you see that on the telly, putting in little screws for electrical fittings, and they all get these little filings in their fingers? They were getting 17p. an hour. They had to work very hard.'

While he was in the Army, Mr Ridout discovered, or someone discovered it for him, that he was mechanically minded and this had interesting results for him at work, where by then the firm had installed machines for knitting fabric gloves.

'We were gradually getting a bit smaller, we didn't have the people, there wasn't enough to do, so Bob Jefferies knew I was mechanically minded, Bob and Mr Spreckley, and they asked me if I'd like to have a look at these machines and I got them going and sorted the problems, and have gone on from there. I would always have liked to have done that sort of thing. I think I would, really. We didn't have the chance in those days, nothing to do in that way. You were lucky if you had an engineer working in the firm. I never had any real training with machinery, just a flair. If you're that way inclined, I think you can do it.'

Fred Ridout got his chance when he was 64. It's quite evident that being a machine mechanic is where his real talents lie, which is another way of saying that for most of his working life he was a square peg in a round hole; a machinery man in an industry that had no use for machinery men. Curiously enough, he was at last able to earn a living as a mechanic at the moment when the British gloving industry began to sense that its future lay with knitted gloves and knitted glove linings, which would be made by machinery, rather than with leather gloves, which demanded skilled hand labour from beginning to end. So the machines and the noise that goes with them have arrived at Warminster and the old-timers, like Fred Ridout and Bob Jefferies, will retire in the middle of what amounts to a revolution in the trade.

Mr Carmen put it this way:

'This is where there is the possibility of the industry reviving. Knitted gloves used to be made by hand in places like Blandford and Fleetwood. It was a craft then. The gloves were knitted by hand. Machinery came in in the 1890s, machines that could make gloves. They didn't knit gloves completely. They made

Dent Allcroft's works at Warminster,
as it was in 1979.

them tubular and somebody would knit the fingers separately by hand. It meant picking up ten or fifteen stitches by hand putting them onto another little machine, a hand machine, which knitted the tubular finger on each hand. This was a labour-intensive industry and it settled down in places like Leicester and Scotland. Then, with the Far Eastern trade coming in, which was very cheap, it all moved over to there. Now the cycle's turned, so that there have been machines invented – we have some of them in the factory – which will actually spit out a glove every $2\frac{1}{2}$ minutes, with all the fingers knitted on, and we are now able to compete with the Koreans, Japanese, and all the rest. This is basically because their wages have gone up, and transport costs have gone up, and the landed prices of gloves in this country are comparable to our own.

'This machine, the one which can produce the whole glove, is a spin-off of the space programme. To retain heat, the Americans had to develop a glove which had to be knitted in one continuous thread. By research they have produced a machine that will actually take one thread and continue to knit the whole glove as one unit, with a metal heating element in it. They weren't allowed to join the thread. The Japanese got hold of this part of the American know-how and they now market these machines very successfully, much to our annoyance, because we ought to be able to buy these machines in Britain. They're exporting all over the world and now we're buying in Japanese machines. The first machine of this type started to be developed commercially about six years ago. We had our first nearly four years ago. It only makes linings in gloves, a woollen glove inside a leather glove, and now we've taken it on and it's turning out somewhere about 400 dozen a week of knitted gloves. We're close to competing with the Far East now, especially since we're getting a measure of protection through the Common Market.'

And so, working only two days a week now, since he had a heart attack when he was 65, Fred Ridout is happy doing his bit to help the industry towards what he sincerely hopes will be a new period of prosperity.

'The doctor, he says, "How do you feel about finishing?" I said, "I don't feel about it at all. I think it's a great mistake." You want some interest, otherwise you finish up like a cabbage. I always think of a fellow I used to work with. He's dead now. He carried on full-time until he was 70. I always thought that was a mistake. Then they said he ought to finish, so he went home and the doctor came to see him, and he said, "You're not working now?" and he said, "No, I had the sack", and the doctor said, "Good job too". He sat down in a chair and within six months he was dead. And he used to do bell-ringing, campanology. Within six months he was dead.

'Honestly, I've got to do something. The funny thing is that I've got a busman's holiday. I've got a knitting machine at home and I knit pullovers. I've had it about ten years. I'd love to get one of the more sophisticated ones, but I knit pullovers and all sorts of other things on it. I don't make anything out of it. If I want a pullover, or a waistcoat, I just knit one. My wife normally does the plain and purl because this machine doesn't do plain and purl. You can do what they call a continental rib, which is leaving every stitch down, and do double length, like they're doing on the gloves here in the factory, turning it up and knitting it on.'

Fred Ridout, as his employers are only too happy to admit, is one of those indispensable people who are always looking for better ways of doing a job, seeing how a machine or a process could be improved. One difficulty with the knitted glove linings was that they tended to flop about, fold over and go out of shape before they could be pressed and finally disciplined. Mr Ridout cudgelled his brains over that one and invented skeleton wire hands on racks that the gloves could be stretched and stored on as they came off the machines, a device that gives the factory a strangely off-beat, surreal appearance, with forests of hands sticking up everywhere.

His obituary could happily be, 'He flowered in his sixties', which is a significant comment on the British gloving industry.

Chapter Five Making aeroplanes

Petter oil engines have been famous since the 1890s. Manufactured until 1939 in Yeovil and since then in Staines and Peterborough, the Petter engine was the foundation of a large and enterprising engineering business, which broadened out in 1915 to include the manufacture of aeroplanes. The aircraft division was eventually hived off to form a separate company, Westland Aircraft, which no longer has any connection with Petters. Since the end of the Second World War, it has concentrated on designing and producing helicopters and is now one of the two or three leading concerns in the world within this field.

In its time, Petters made, besides their celebrated oil engines, motorcars, tractors, the Nautilus grate and adding machines. They also lit the entire town of Yeovil from their own works generating station. Their involvement with aircraft came about in the following way. In 1915 Lloyd George said in Parliament that Britain was facing a very serious munitions problem. Petters accordingly wrote to the War Office and the Admiralty, placing their entire manufacturing resources at the disposal of the Government. Soon afterwards, they were informed that the Navy were in urgent need of sea-planes and so, with absolutely no experience of making aeroplanes of any kind, they agreed to take on the contract. A site was acquired on the outskirts of Yeovil, with a railway running along one side, buildings were rapidly erected and by the time of the Armistice 1,100 aircraft of various types had been built there – Short seaplanes, two-seater fighters, mainly DH–4s and DH–9s, and, towards the end of the war, two fighter types designed by Westlands themselves, the single-seater Wagtail and the two-seater Weasel.

During the Twenties, the company kept going with such military orders as were available and with experimental work, including Pterodactyl IV, a tailless cabin aeroplane. In 1934 the organisation of the Aircraft Works was considerably modified. R. A. Bruce, who had been in charge from its early beginnings,

Petters. The foundation of the business. 'Handyman' oil engine, 1907.

Petters. The Nautilus Works, Yeovil, now the bus garage. Built in 1900, this was the firm's main engineering establishment until the move to Loughborough in 1938.

Birdseye view of the Nautilus Works, Yeovil, England.

CONTENTS.

left the Company and the factory was considerably extended and modernised, 'in order to meet the heavy production demands caused by the present emergency conditions of increasing the Royal Air Force'.

R. B. Brigham joined Westlands in 1929, before the re-organisation and expansion. He had been apprenticed to Black-burns, in Leeds, in 1915, spent two years with the Royal Flying Corps and then returned to complete his apprenticeship. Shortly afterwards he left to become an inspector with Vickers, who had the contract to build the R.100 airship. He worked with Nevil Shute on this and well remembers Shute's terrible stammer and how irritated Shute was by it. When the R.100 was completed, Brigham answered an advertisement for a Chief Inspector with Westlands and got the job.

'In those days the aircraft section consisted of approximately four hundred people. We were then turning out Wapitis, and I came as Chief Inspector down here. I never thought I was going to get the job, because there were people older than me in for it. Mr R. A. Bruce, the Managing Director, and his son-in-law, Captain Keep, interviewed me. Captain Keep was the Company's Chief Test Pilot before he lost both his legs in a flying accident. After he lost his legs he became Deputy Managing Director, because his father-in-law was the Managing Director. He was a very nice man. Of course, in those days you weren't allowed to smoke in the factory, the only person allowed to smoke there was R. A. Bruce. If you wanted R. A. Bruce you had to follow him, follow the smell, because he used to smoke Turkish cigarettes and, as the smell got stronger, you would find R. A. Bruce.

'The buildings were pretty basic. We weren't a big firm, you see. We had what we called the Vimy shop where they built Vimys during the war. We had a coppersmith's, a tin-basher's, and that sort of thing. But, of course, don't forget these planes were still wood and string and fabric. There was a dope shop and a paint shop.

'I was paid £400 a year when I arrived and, apart from the Chief Designer, I was about the second highest paid man in the factory. Then we fell on stony ground for a few months. I had just got married, and we had a salary cut of £50. Mr R. A. Bruce went to America for three months and gave some instructions before he went. He said, "I want you to organise and build for me a rib-testing apparatus", and so I got this rib-testing machine designed. I got it made, I got the fellows to make it, all the linkages and everything like that. When Mr Bruce came back from the States, he always used to wander around rubbing his hands, and he said, "Now then Brigham, have you got anything to show me?" So I said, "Yes, sir, I've got a rib-testing machine with a rib in it ready for testing." "Good for you, let's

Westland Aircraft Limited. Main erecting shop in the late Twenties. The shops were lit entirely by gas at this time.

go and see it tested." And by the grace of God and a fair breeze, it worked perfectly. About two hours later he called me back into his office and said, "I've put that £50 back on your salary."

'Mr Bruce had gone to America to study the American management and production methods. When he came back he had the American idea of everybody, management and everybody, starting at eight o'clock in the morning. You had to have a clock card. The senior people hadn't had that sort of thing before. We'd always started at eight o'clock, but we never had a clock card. The juniors did, the work people did, of course, and the draughtsmen did. The first day this was organised I went to find my clock card and there wasn't one, so I never clocked on, but Bill Gibson, who was the Works Manager, he used to tickle me to death. He used to come down without a shave, he used to go and punch his card and then go home for his breakfast. But the system didn't last for more than three months.'

In the Twenties and Thirties, when millions were out of work, Westlands continued to be very busy and Yeovil was a prosperous place. But without military orders Westlands would

have been in a bad way. They produced a number of prototypes which the aviation people thought were brilliant designs, way ahead of their time, but none of them really got anywhere, mainly because they never got any Government backing. It was a fiercely competitive period, with between twenty and thirty aircraft factories all busy designing aeroplanes to meet Government specifications, knowing that most of them were going to fail to win contracts. It was a wasteful system; at any given time the RAF might be operating as many as ten different types of aircraft, all from different manufacturers.

In the non-military field, Westlands built a passenger aircraft, called the Wessex, which, with six orders, was their best sale. So the factory's bread-and-butter always came from supplying the world's air forces. The main product between 1925 and 1935 was the Wapiti. It was a general purpose aeroplane and at one time there were more RAF squadrons equipped with Wapitis than with any other make. The South African and Australian Air Forces adopted the Wapiti as their standard machine.

Five Wapitis a week were being completed when Mr

Brigham arrived in Yeovil. It was originally a wood and canvas affair, but it was eventually redesigned as an all-metal aeroplane. About 1,200 were eventually produced, which, for a peacetime aircraft, was an exceptionally large number. And at the same time a great deal of research and development was going on with monoplanes. It was a busy period and an overhaul of the management structure was inevitable.

'Mr R. A. Bruce retired, and Captain Acland came as Managing Director. We used to call him "bum and eyeglass". He was a hell of a fellow. He didn't know anything about being a Managing Director; he knew a lot about rugby, though. He was a rugby man. But he was all right to get on with, we got on fine with him.

'It was during the slump, and Bill Gibson, the Works Manager, wanted a lot more men, he wanted another 150 or a couple of hundred. We couldn't get them. Bill Gibson, Captain Acland and myself were in Acland's office, and Bill Gibson said, "I can't get the men", and like a fool – I was a Yorkshire man, you see – I said, "You're not bloody well trying". And Acland said, "Right, can you get them?" I said, sticking my neck out, "Yes." So he said, "Go and get 'em." So I made an arrangement to go to the various Labour Exchanges in Coventry, Birmingham, Sheffield, Leeds, Durham, Newcastle, North Shields, South Shields, and the results were amazing. I got 175 people. They weren't skilled aircraft people, I got ship's engineers, I got pattern makers, I got good blokes, and some of them hadn't worked for eight years. When you went into the Labour Exchange, they came up with their green card, you interviewed them, and then you had to put your hand in your pocket and say, "Now then, what was your bus fare this morning?". And they said, "Bus fare?" And I said again, "How much is your bus fare?" And the man would say, "I've no idea. We don't get a bus, you know." Some of these fellows hardly had shoes on their feet. I said, "Well, how far have you come?" And one man said, "Eight miles."

'This was in 1931. In those days the Labour Exchange took their green cards, if you engaged men, and paid them their fares down to Yeovil, and then they gave them so much maintenance, I think it was for twelve weeks, something like that, and then if they fitted in well they would help them in obtaining a council house. That's how we got the men to build a hell of a lot of aircraft.'

The 175 men that Mr Brigham recruited among the unemployed in the Midlands and North nearly all stayed put in Yeovil.

'In the old days, you know, you walked round the factory and you knew everybody – Bill, or Charlie, or whatever he was – and you could go and chat to them. When I was retiring, fellows were coming up to me and they'd say, "Mr Brigham, you don't remember me, but you brought me down from South Shields". A bloke came in to me when I was in South Shields and he said, "Can I bring my mate in?" I said, "Yes, by all means". They came in, and I said, "How long have you been out of work?" He said, "A fortnight". I said, "A fortnight? You want to go in an aircraft factory?" He said, "Yes, please. We're good tradesmen, you know." So I said, "Well, if you've got second class tickets, I think you must be good tradesmen, but why the hell do you want to leave the sea and go into an aircraft factory?" And he said, "Have you ever been to Hong Kong in a bloody 9-knot boat? It takes you a hell of a long time. You don't half get bored." And I started those two, and they stayed here, I expect they're retired now, like me.'

Not that all the men at Westlands came from the old industrial areas. When Petters moved their oil-engine business to Loughborough, many of their employees preferred to stay where they were, much to Mr Brigham's delight.

'Believe me, if you've got a Petters man you've got a craftsman. You've got a damned good craftsman, because they were taught their job at Petters. There were quite a lot that wouldn't go to Loughborough. They'd got their homes here, and after all, who the hell wants to go to Loughborough, one of the coldest places in England?'

In due course the War arrived and Westlands found themselves working seven days a week, twenty-four hours a day. And one day Mr Brigham had a considerable surprise.

'I was sat in my office one Sunday morning – we were working Sundays then – and my secretary said, "Lord Beaverbrook on the phone". I said, "Don't talk daft, Lord Beaverbrook doesn't know me". She said, "Well, he says he's Lord Beaverbrook". Anyway, I answered the phone and it was the Beaver, and he said, "Brigham?" I didn't know whether to say "Yes, sir" or "Yes, my lord", or what. He said, "I want you to report to me at half-past nine at Millbank tomorrow morning". I said, "Wait a minute, Lord Beaverbrook, I just don't happen to be working for you, I'm working for Sir Eric Mensforth". He said, "Put me through to Mensforth". So I put him through to Mensforth, and about five minutes later in came Mensforth into my office, and said, "Brigham, don't you realise there's a war on?" I said, "I realise as much as anybody else there's a war on, why?" He said, "You've had a command". I said, "I've had a request by Lord Beaverbrook to be at Millbank at half-past nine in the morning".

Lord Beaverbrook was the Minister of Aircraft Production and at that time, after the great Winston Churchill himself, probably the most powerful man in Britain, so to anyone in the aeroplane business, a call from Beaverbrook was a call from

God himself, as Sir Eric lost no time in impressing on Mr Brigham.

'He said, "You've got to go". So I said, "Well, what do I do, what do I want to go up there for?" He said, "I don't know, but you report to Lord Beaverbrook at half-past nine at Millbank". So of course I packed my little bag and I went to Millbank. I was ushered in to Lord Beaverbrook, and another bloke came in, and he said, "Take Brigham's photograph". I thought, "What's all this about?" "Now, Brigham," Beaverbrook said, "I've got a job for you, I want you to go and produce the Hurricanes." I said, "Me? I don't think I've ever seen a Hurricane". He said, "You've got to go and produce these Hurricanes. I've had you highly recommended to me as the man to do the job." I don't know who the hell had recommended me. So I had my photograph taken, they gave me a special pass, and he said, "You will have a through line on the telephone to anywhere in the country, and I want you to report to me every Wednesday morning to know the progress you're making." So I said, "What progress has been made?" He said, "At the present, none. You've got to alter that."

'It was damned funny, to tell the truth. I walked into the Managing Director's office at Kingston-on-Thames – it was the Hawker Siddeley factory – and he said, "Brigham, I suppose? You're not welcome." I said, "Well, I didn't bloody well want to come". So he said, "Well, you're not welcome". And after that he said, "If you stay, I go." I said, "Well, it's a bit of an impasse, isn't it? Can I have Franklin 2211?" He gave me the phone and I got the Beaver. I said to him, "Look, there's a bit of an impasse here, Lord Beaverbrook. If I stay, the Managing Director's going." So he said, "Put me on to Sutton." So I gave Sutton the phone and said, "He wants to talk to you now." Sutton put the phone down, picked up his umbrella and his bowler hat and walked out. And there was I, stuck in the Managing Director's office, all on my own. I thought, "I've got to find somebody here, find a secretary or something." I got the secretary – I hadn't been to Kingston in my life before – and I said, "Look, will you give me the names of the senior management in this organisation? Will you type them out for me, please?" I told her my name was Brigham, and what I was there for. She said, "If you like, come into my office, I'll type them out straight away and give you their titles." So I did, and I said, "Now I'd like to see everybody on this list at nine o'clock in the morning in the Board Room." I went in the Board Room at nine o'clock with this wench, and only two people turned up. So I said, "Where the hell is everybody?" She said, "Well, you see, Mr Brigham, it's not usual for them to come until half past nine." I said, "But there's a war on. Look, will you send word

round that I want to see everyone on this list at nine o'clock in the Board Room tomorrow morning." And that's how I got busy with Hurricanes. Lord Beaverbrook gave me an inscribed gold watch at the end of it. I've still got it, but it doesn't go now.'

In 1936, just after the great reorganisation took place at Westlands, Mr F. L. Swain came to the Yeovil factory from Manchester. He answered an advertisement for an Inspector and he got the job. At that time, they were making the famous Wapiti and a developed form of it called the Wallace.

'They had a contract for 500 Wapitis when I came, and they had a hundred still to make, and then they got a contract for 50 Wallaces, which, incidentally, was the first military aeroplane with an enclosed cockpit. The next contract after that was to build under licence a machine that was manufactured by Hawkers, called a Hawker Hector, and we built about 160-odd of those. From that we went on to the Lysander, at the beginning of the war. It seemed a very prosperous firm to me, but what I couldn't get over, coming from Manchester, was going out every day into a factory in the middle of the fields and woods. This was the thing that struck me most. Another thing was the people. I thought when I arrived, "My God, there's half of Lancashire down here." And there was. There were a lot of North Country people down here.

'I nearly didn't stay. I was single, you see, and to tell you the truth I had an up and downer with the Deputy Chief Inspector, and I said "Well, this is no good to me, I'm going back," and that was after six weeks. But I didn't go back. I met my wife and married eighteen months afterwards, and that was it. But I still had at the back of my mind that I would leave after the war. But then I became acclimatised to Yeovil, which I must admit took a bit of doing. It took me a long time to know the people. Up North there's a totally different type of people. You talk to somebody on the bus up there. Here you could go into a pub and you wouldn't speak to anyone all the evening.

'I thought it was a reasonably efficient place. It wasn't the hustle and bustle of the North, but work got done. I suppose Brigham was the bloke I had most to do with, and he always struck me as being nothing exceptional but quite a fair bloke. I wouldn't have classified him as an ace or anything like that, but to be fair, there weren't many aces in the management, anywhere.'

Nowadays, Westlands have an excellent apprenticeship scheme but, when Mr Swain came in 1936, he found quite a different state of affairs. 'I think,' he said, 'in those days, if there were twenty apprentices, that was as many as there were.' So the reason why Westlands had to go round the country buying in skilled men was that they simply weren't producing enough

Mr Brigham's war-time responsibilities. Workshops in Westland's subsidiary factory at Sherborne. The photograph is marked 'Secret'.

Mr Brigham's war-time responsibilities. The wing-shop at Chard. Also 'Secret'.

of their own. And that seemed to Mr Swain to have been a major management failure.

In the period between the wars, however, when most engineering firms found the going hard, there was a general shortage of apprenticeships. Training was something that management felt it could cut down on, as a way of saving money. Westlands were not exceptionally bad or shortsighted in this respect. Mr Swain had experienced the problem at first-hand.

'I was an apprentice with Guest, Keen and Nettlefolds and I was what they called a pupil apprentice. My father paid some money for me to go and do a metallurgical engineer's course. There again, it was only because he knew a chap in Guest, Keen's that I got in. There was a lot of that in those days.'

In the Thirties, he believed, most men came down to Westlands from the North, the Midlands and London with the intention of staying only two or three years until times improved and then going back. But most of them eventually decided to settle permanently in Yeovil, and the main reason for that, he believes, was the unusually pleasant atmosphere at the works.

'One of the happiest places that I know. I've been in some big engineering plants and at Westlands there was certainly a very happy family atmosphere all the way through. People grew up with the firm and stayed with it. The people who've done over twenty-five years with the company, every year they have a social, and they present gold watches to everyone who's arrived at twenty-five years. There's over 1,200 attend it, that's retired people and people who've done twenty-five years, so that's quite something.'

Mr Swain doesn't believe this friendly atmosphere was an accident. 'It seemed to be a fellowship that was created. What created it I can't tell you. It was there when I came. I felt it. I was attracted to the people from my own part of the country, but even so, it was there. It was a real family affair.'

A key figure in this, he believes, was Ted Wheeldon, who ended his career with Westlands as Chairman of the Company.

'Ted Wheeldon created a good atmosphere in that firm. There was always a liaison between him when he was the Chairman and, say, the fellow who swept the lavatories out. If that man wanted to see Wheeldon, and Wheeldon thought he had to see him, he'd see him.

'He was a trained engineer. He was trained at the Metropolitan Vickers electrical works at Trafford Park, Manchester. He was an apprentice there and as an apprentice he was quite good. He was eventually moved up into a semi-management position on the costing side. At that time the Managing Director of Metropolitan Vickers was Aubrey Mensforth, who later became Sir Aubrey Mensforth, and his son, Eric Mensforth, became the Managing Director of Westlands during the war. So Wheeldon was pushed on by the Mensforths. When he came from Trafford Park two years after I did, in 1938, he came as superintendent of one of the shops. He progressed up the ladder to Works Manager, Works Director, Managing Director, Deputy Chief Executive and finally, about four years before he retired, he was Chairman of the Company. He was a practical man and he was stern and rigid for protocol, but at the same time he had a soft side to him. People knew if anything went wrong, any hitch in industrial relations, he would put it right. It can't be an accident that there was never one strike at Westlands while he was there.'

But there have been several since and, in Mr Swain's opinion, this may well be not unconnected with the enormous growth of the company since 1945. In 1957 the Government decided that it would be generally beneficial if the British aircraft industry reorganised itself into a small number of groups. With this official encouragement, Westlands bought Saunders-Roe in 1959, acquiring in this way that company's helicopter interests and the SR-N1 hovercraft; the helicopter division of the Bristol Aeroplane Company in 1960; and, also in 1960, the Fairey Aviation Company, which was working on VTOL transport aircraft.

In human terms, this can be translated into 4,000 employees before the take-overs and 11,500 in 1968. Greater size inevitably brought more problems in industrial relations. Neither Westlands nor the aircraft industry were peculiar in this. Whatever former employees may say about shortcomings in management and organisation, the plain fact is that a concern with 4,000 people is easier to run than one with 11,000. Those who are fortunate enough to have known the company before it became big inevitably feel nostalgic about the old days, when the Managing Director spent much of his time walking about the works and knew everybody by name, or so the legend goes. The bigger a firm becomes, the more remote the workers are bound to be from the top management, and very special skills and insight are required to deal with this state of affairs. The important factor is not necessarily what the situation really is, but what people feel and believe it to be.

But, to a certain extent, Mr Swain was insulated from the post-war changes at Westlands. While he was in the Inspection Department, he had also acted as the Department's technical representative, and in 1946 he began travelling round the world full-time. 'Alan Bristow was the pilot, I was his grease monkey', and whenever and wherever Westlands sold helicopters, Bristow and Swain were there to show the customers how to handle them and how to look after them. One of the first jobs they had together was to go over to France with the helicopters that had been bought to spray the potato fields against the Colorado beetle.

Westlands has been a much written about company and anyone whose main interest is technical, that is, aircraft manufacturing and design, will have no great problem in finding the details he needs. This does not add up to the history of a company, however. The kind of information provided by Mr Brigham and Mr Swain is an essential supplement and corrective to the official record. For fairly obvious reasons, it does not normally find its way into print. Few companies, inside or outside the aircraft industry, are happy that the world shall see them as they really are or were. The historian needs the Mr Brighams and Mr Swains very badly.

Chapter Six   Making biscuits

The British have been great biscuit eaters for more than a century and a half, which is another way of saying that they have been great biscuit makers for a long time. The leading Victorian firms – Huntley and Palmer, Peek Frean, Jacobs, McVitie and Price – were known throughout the world. The variety and quality of the biscuits these household names produced were part of the British way of life. Biscuits were the most important snack for generations before potato crisps were even thought of, but in recent years they have lost ground to the newer nibbles and the industry, although still of considerable size, has declined from the heights it reached in the inter-war period. Nearly all the formerly independent firms have been absorbed into two large groups. Production has been centralised, factories sold off and demolished, new and more efficient premises erected. Twenty years ago, no British patriot would have believed that biscuit making could ever come to an end in Reading, where Huntley and Palmer's empire had seemed as firmly established and eternal as the British monarchy. But the factories, for so long a vast advertisement by the side of the main railway line to Paddington, baked their last biscuit in 1977 and a large part of the buildings have now been pulled down, with only an office block and some warehouses to keep the name of Huntley and Palmer alive after Associated Biscuits Ltd had swallowed the business alive and whole.

Mrs Eleanor Coller went to work at Peek Frean's in Bermondsey in 1928, when she was fifteen. She left school on her fourteenth birthday and started work the next day at a shirt factory. After a little over a year with shirts, she decided she needed a change and moved over to biscuits for eight months, during the factory's rush period. The job came to an end and she returned to her original factory as a shirt presser and stayed there until she married four years later.

At Peek Frean, she was what was known in the trade as a biscuit creamer. Each biscuit received individual treatment.

'There were about eight girls to a long bench and on the bench we had tools very much like the ones the ice-cream man used to hold when he was making an ice-cream wafer. We held one biscuit in this little piece of equipment, spread the cream mixture on it with a wooden spatula – we had to scoop the cream from a large vat into a basin – and then topped it off with another biscuit, making sure that the two biscuits matched one another in shade. If they didn't, you had them back to do again.

'Some of the biscuits had jam as well as cream in them. There was a hole in the top biscuit and you put strawberry jam into it. We got the hot jam from a large vat, put it into an icing bag and then piped the jam into the hole.

'Christmas fancy biscuits were made by hand, too. You had a piece of wood, which you dipped into the coloured icing, spread it on the biscuit and then laid the biscuits on wire trays.

'Whenever biscuits were for export, we always had to make sure that they were dark in colour, because they faded during the sea journey.

'We started work at eight and went on until six, Mondays to Fridays. On Saturdays, the hours were ten to one. And for that I got ten shillings a week. Nobody else in my family had ever worked at Peek Frean's.

'For the time, I suppose working conditions at Peek Frean's were quite good. The discipline was strict, though. We had to be scrupulously clean. Our hands and our clothes were inspected by a forelady each time we entered the room where we worked. They made sure we hadn't any pins on us and we weren't allowed to wear rings or jewellery of any kind.

'I worked under very bad conditions as a shirt and pyjama presser. Each shirt had to be ironed by hand and pinned ready for the shop. It was sweated labour. The piece-work rates were very low, but beggars can't be choosers. I should have liked to stay at Peek Frean's, but there wasn't a job there for me.

'We could buy biscuits there very cheaply, especially broken ones, but when you worked among biscuits all day long, you didn't really want them. If you stole biscuits, you were in trouble. We could be called into the office at any gate to be searched. They had women there to do that. Anyway, it didn't cross your mind to take things. You just knew it was wrong. You behaved, you accepted things.

'I'm glad I lived in those days. It was all hard work, but I considered myself very lucky, and I still do.'

Mrs Coller worked in the mass market part of the biscuit trade, and it is interesting to compare her experiences with those of people employed by a small firm making a semi-luxury biscuit.

The Bath Oliver is as famous a British product as the Digestive biscuit. Wherever the British Empire extended, there

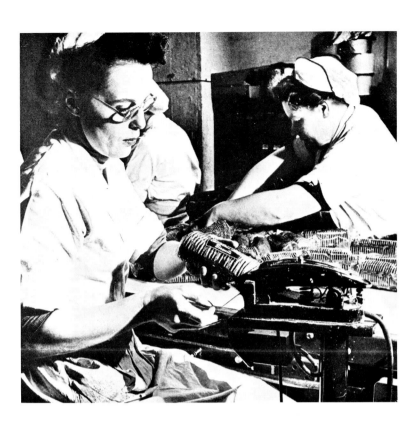

Girls on the production line at Peek Frean in the 1950s.

were Bath Olivers. Lord Roberts ate them regularly, to help defeat the Boers, and a Ugandan chief had crate-loads of them sent to the coast and carried 600 miles overland by bearers to his village. The story of this biscuit is almost part of the nation's folklore. Invented by Dr William Oliver, who was appointed physician to the Royal Mineral Water Hospital in Bath in 1740, it was intended in the first place as part of the treatment prescribed to his well-to-do patients who were ill from over-eating and over-drinking. Originally made by Dr Oliver in the kitchen of his house at Bathford, it was baked after his death by Atkins, his trusted coachman, on a more commercial scale. The recipe and the right to manufacture were sold successively to four other people during the next hundred years and then came into the hands of James Fortt, first in the line of the well-known Bath family of food manufacturers, who had the reputation of making the best Bath buns in the city, at a time when Bath buns were really worth eating.

James Fortt made the biscuits on the site of Atkins' premises at 13 Green Street, but when his son, W. E. Fortt, took over in the 1870s, the business was transferred to a corner shop in Broad Street. There was a legend, almost certainly untrue, that only the inventor and the current principal of the bakery were supposed to know the secret ingredient that gave the Olivers their special quality. However, the recipe was certainly a closely guarded secret and all the people working for Fortts were sworn to secrecy.

The original method of making the biscuits involved a great deal of hard labour. The dough was rolled through a kind of mangle to bring it to the required thickness; each biscuit was cut out individually with a hand cutter and placed face to face in pairs to be 'docked', that is, to have a pattern of holes punched in it. The biscuits were then gently taken apart and put face upward on the baking tin, so that the perforation stood up. The point of the docking process was to provide air holes to prevent the biscuit rising while it was in the oven.

In 1900 Fortts built a large new factory near the railway station in Manvers Street. The output at that time was 70,000 biscuits a day and the new premises were arranged for making bread and cakes as well as biscuits. Production was to a large extent mechanised and the system was that the biscuits were baked during the day and bread at night.

The factory was badly damaged by a bomb in 1942, but it was rapidly repaired and rebuilt. Raw materials for the Olivers were difficult or impossible to get during the war years, and the plant was given over to much more utilitarian kinds of biscuits, especially for the Army and Navy. After the war, the factory never completely returned to normal. The Fortt family and

Rear of Fortt's Bath Oliver factory, Manvers Street, Bath. Early 1900s.

Factory.
Back
View.

96

their partners, the Stoffells, had no sons to take over the business and in 1961 it was sold to what was at that time Huntley and Palmers and the factory in Bath subsequently demolished, to make room for the headquarters of the Bath and Portland Group. Bath Olivers were made in Reading until 1977, when production was transferred to Sir Harold Wilson's constituency at Huyton in Lancashire, from where the familiar packets now come.

Few biscuits can have had quite such an adventurous history and few people lived with Bath Olivers as long as Mr Reuben Weekes, who went to Manvers Street in 1921 for twelve shillings a week at the age of fourteen, and stayed there until 1957. For twenty of those years he was what he describes as 'the charge hand on biscuits'. Mr Weekes has his own delightfully old-fashioned, rather Irish form of chronology. When he was asked when he first went to the Bath Oliver factory, he said, 'I went there just after the fire'. Now the fire, a particularly disastrous one, was in 1919 but, like Cromwell's behaviour in Ireland, it was such an awe-inspiring event and made such a deep impression on all who witnessed it and knew about it that it was natural to use it as a fixed point in discussing time. The factory was restored to production, but Fortts were not adequately insured and never really recovered from the blow to their finances. The Stoffells were brought in as partners to provide the money needed to set the business on its feet again. 'The fire', within the business, had something of the catastrophic quality of the Great Fire of London about it. It was not something to be referred to lightly.

Reuben Weekes tells the story in his own characteristic way.

'It was a tragedy. Harry Wheeler's father worked there and he came there after me as a boy. His father died years ago. But Harry told me someone was walking up through the bakehouse with a piece of lighted paper, to light the gas. There used to be a little lift and when they had the old peel ovens, the boy's job was to slide in the biscuits in the baskets and to put the wicker baskets into this little hand lift and pull a rope to take them up to the packing room, upstairs. They reckon somebody was coming up with a piece of paper and the lift was gone up, and this paper with the upward draught went up and of course it was all wood up there, old wooden staircase and everything, and it went like a bomb. This is hearsay, mind, but I was told the Fortts were under-insured, that's what happened. There was no Caters, Caters were dead, but they traded under the name of Cater, Stoffell and Fortt, it was only Stoffells. I suppose they must have got together and said, "We want to try and re-open the factory", and they went in with Stoffells. Stoffells took the controlling interest and that was a bad thing, because Stoffells were grocers, you see, and they didn't know a lot about the

Forwarding
Room.

Corner of
Store
Room.

98

baking trade. Even as a boy I could see that. And that was how they came to be in along with Fortts. Old man Stoffell, when I used to remember him, he came down and he saw me smoking one day in the yard in my dinner hour, and he said, "Don't you smoke, my son, you won't grow". I was a young man then, nearly nineteen. Then Claude used to come up and down, but William Ernest Fortt was there, he was what I call a silly gentleman, he used to let things slip away, he was out on the golf course. Anyhow, they got rid of him in the finish. Harold stopped, you remember Harold Fortt? Nice old bloke. I got on very well with Harold, and he knew me like a book. I used to go up and see him just before he died, in his flat. That was what actually happened.'

When Mr Weekes went there at the impressionable age of fourteen, only the best ingredients were going into Bath Olivers.

'We were making nine sacks a day. Now a sack of biscuits is 280 lb of flour, plus the pure butter. I used to see this go in as a kid, I used to help weigh it, pure lard, malt extract and full cream milk supplied by the Abbey Dairy, honestly.'

In those days, the 'malt extract' was made on the premises.

'We used to go round to Widcombe, which was a free house, they used to supply us with all the grain and the hops, you see, for us to brew with. I used to brew a lot, you know. We used to put this grain in big wooden oak tubs and the hops with it, and then when the sponge was put on, we used to use so much of that, but they had a big copper container there, and used to use so much hops, so much malt grain, put it in, and that had to be brought up. The malt was brought right up to the boil and then there was a big round skimmer, you used to go along and skim all the scum off and after you skimmed it you put the lid back on and you had to turn the gas down low and that had to be kept going like that for exactly five hours.

'Old Bert Pitman, the engineer there, poor old Bert, he's dead and gone now. When he couldn't get a pint he'd go down and pinch some of this and, of course, it was deadly. A couple of times they found him up the wall, poor old Bert, and he'd be down at this brew. The only thing was, Bert didn't care about that, but there was no sugar in it. I think old Bert used to pinch some and put a bit of sugar in it, if he didn't have the money for a pint, see. He used to go over the Railway then, I can remember him well as a boy. He used to put so many pints on the slate. Of course, when he got too many up they wouldn't let him have any more, and as soon as his wages come on the Saturday – we never used to get paid until Saturday – he used to have to go and pay what he owed on the slate, and poor old Bert, he never hardly had any money to take home. But they were all the same. But what did they have? There was no wireless, there was no television.'

New Factory Entrance.

The Ram Brewery at Widcombe was not exactly a brewery in the way we use the word today. It was, in fact, a pub that brewed its own beer. By then, there were only three pubs in the Bath area that carried on the old tradition of brewing for themselves, and the Ram was closest to the biscuit factory. It also happened to be the place that supplied the baking men with the beer the firm allowed them to buy. And fetching the beer allowance was a job for the boy, which meant, for a while, Reuben Weekes.

'Old Jim Lane, he used to have six pints, you see, used to ignore everyone else. And beer was 4d., 5d. and 6d. then. Well, some used to have fourpenny, some used to have fivepenny, and some used to have sixpenny. Old Jim, he used to have sixpenny, and one day I brought it back and I must have had the bottles mixed up, they were heavy, in a big wicker basket. I used to go up to old Jim first, running in sweat, and say, "Here you are, Jim", and old Jim knew his own bottles. I must have got them mixed somehow, and another, because old Jim wasn't too pleased about it. I've seen old Jim tip the bottle up and it's run out of his mouth. This day I must have mixed the bottles up – he had a hand on him like a leg of pork, great big arms, great big hands – and he said, "That's not my b . . . bottle". So I used to get some sticky paper after that and stick on Jim's six bottles, so I didn't get them mixed up. I laugh when I look back on it, but they were hard days.'

By the time Reuben Weekes arrived at the age of fourteen, the demand for Bath Olivers had grown to the point where the existing oven couldn't cope. So the great bakery experts, Baker Perkins of Peterborough, were called in, to see if there was any way in which the baking process could be speeded up from the 40–45 minutes it was taking at that time. Baker Perkins sent their Mr Alcock and experiment after experiment was carried out, with the young Weekes anxious to lend a hand whenever possible, for the most necessary of reasons.

'They had a hell of a job, but every time he would have me on this oven, Mr Alcock, he was a real old gent, and every time I went on the ovens he used to give me ten bob. Of course, that was a vast amount of money in those days. They used to say, "Mr Alcock's coming", so I used to try and push myself in, and he'd say to me, "Are you coming on the travelling oven for me, my son?" and every time he'd finished, and it took them thirty or forty times to get it right, and every time he gave me half a quid. My money was twelve bob, you see, so if you got a ten bob tip, it was vast.'

Towards the end, Mr Weekes found things getting pretty chaotic and he decided to call it a day and leave.

'I left there, because we got in such a state, chaps kept leaving for better wages, you see, and they got less and less and less, and

Fortt's factory. The main entrance, showing the famous shop. An exhaustive search resulted in only one collection of illustrations relating to the factory, that in the possession of Mrs Betty Summers, whose father, Mr Albert Fussell, spent his whole working life with the firm. The photographs are so rare that one has to pardon the occasional lapses in the matter of quality.

Mr Albert Fussell in the Twenties.

we were on biscuits, we were a separate entity from confectionery. They split us off. The new manager that came split us off.
We were working from half past seven to half past five at night,
and then the chaps kept leaving and they said, "Will you give a
hand on confectionery?" which I had done since I was a boy, and
knew a little bit about it. So first of all they said, "Come in
at half past six", and then it was six, then it was half past five
and in the finish it was half past four in the morning. Well, that

e right the wonder machine which presses the dough into long narrow strips and passes it through another portion of the machine which cuts it into dock." This machine is the only one of its kind in the world. Two stages in biscuit making in a Bath factory.

Mr Fussell, third from left, at work.

meant getting up at half past three. I used to go and give a hand on all the small ones, until about half past seven, quarter to eight, and have half an hour's break and then go and start your biscuits. You didn't know what time you were going to finish.'

And he has a strong suspicion that nowadays his beloved Olivers aren't what they used to be, secret recipe or no secret recipe. A year or two ago his wife bought him a tin to try. He thought straight away that the colour was too pale.

'She brought them along here and I looked at them. I can remember an Oliver biscuit when it was a lovely pale yellow colour, and that was the lard that did that, they used to shine on the top. Old George used to call it the bloom. Used to say, "got a nice bloom on them". But then the ingredients that went in, you see. Those were the days they used to pack all their Bath buns in boxes and they used to say, "If it's Fortts, it's good", that was their slogan. And by God, it *was* good.'

The difficulty is, of course, that one can't prove it either way, because, so far as we know, no pre-war Olivers have survived to make any sort of scientific comparison possible. But it may well be as Reuben Weekes says, although there is just a hope that a pre-war tin of Bath Olivers may turn up one day to confuse the issue.

Leonard Haines joined the firm at the same time as Reuben Weekes did, but as an older man. He was Chief Clerk at the factory for thirty years and he was particularly concerned with distribution. Nowadays most of the biscuits are sold in packets, but until comparatively recently there were always tall round tins and, in Mr Haines' view, this was a sensible way of going about the job.

'The policy of having round tins paid. They're airtight. We used to put the tape all round there, to be on the safe side. Those biscuits would last for years, you see. I've tasted some thirty or forty years old. We had a code on there, you see. That would tell us what month it was made in, and the year.'

Mr Haines worked for the firm in the days when nearly everything was shipped away by rail. Bath at that time was served by two railways, the LMS and the Great Western, each with its own goods depôt.

'Both the railways used to collect our biscuits every night. We used to send off every day of the week, bar Saturdays, in our own boxes, which were returnable, you see. We had boxes taking a dozen, two dozen, three dozen. The railway companies called themselves, both of them, every evening – the LMS (London, Midlands and Scottish Railways) and the Great Western. That was part of my job, to mark every order which way it had to go. The railway companies would call in the evening, after four o'clock, and the LMS would take their share and the Great Western would take theirs. The local stuff, like Bristol, we used to take ourselves in the van.'

Margaret Walters belongs to a much younger generation than Mr Weekes or Mr Haines. She started work in Manvers Street in 1958, straight from school.

'I went there in the office, I was only fourteen then. I shouldn't have been there. They took me on, but when the manager, Mr Allen, found out my birthday was in September, I had to leave. So I went into printing, and I thought, "I'll go back there". Although it was a factory, it was very small and I liked it.

'I didn't go into the biscuit department, I went straight down into despatch on the ground floor. There was Lily Banks, and a friend of mine I still keep in contact with. There was just the three of us there. I was put on this packing machine, packing all the cakes, the big cakes for the shops, and putting up orders for shops. They were all local shops.

'The cakes, the majority of them, anyway, were made at night-time. During the day all the fondant and the fillings and all that sort of thing had to be done, but the actual basic cakes were done at night. They would make the sponge at night and in the day they used to ice them. They used to go out the next morning. We used to put up orders in the morning, so there was something to do all day. I was more on the packing side of it, the Swiss rolls, and the madeira fruit, all the bigger cakes, the Battenbergs. The fancy cakes were prepared more upstairs.

They came down to us to be despatched the next morning.

'There were about eight or ten people working on the confectionery side, upstairs. I came in contact with the girls on the biscuits, but I didn't actually work with the biscuits, I didn't sit on the conveyor with the girls and help pack. On the middle floor, that was. But I do remember them experimenting with chocolate Olivers.

'When they first came to start doing it there was a little tiny room next to the mechanics' place, very tiny, and they set it up in there. This was a much smaller Oliver biscuit, and I can remember the chocolate kept coming off the Oliver because it was too hard. Then they got fridges in and all that. I didn't know from that day to this whether they did get it off the ground. I know they were very expensive and the chocolate used to go white on them. They spent hours, the management, with this young girl who was in it all on her own, dipping the biscuits by hand into all this chocolate and putting them in trays, trying to keep them cool as well. She had all these fans down there, and it was all so exciting. I don't know whether or not they continued with it. I think it stopped while I was there.'

The chocolate Oliver presents the historian with a difficult problem, which illustrates the great care that has to be taken with the interpretation of people's memories of their work. Fortts made chocolate-covered Olivers long before the Second World War. What, then, was the 'experimenting' that was going on in the Fifties? Another of our informants, Mrs Betty Summers, provides the information that helps us to find the answer. This is her description of how the job was done in 1935, when she started work in the factory after leaving school.

Chocolate Olivers were only produced on Mondays, which made them unpopular with the girls, because the chocolate used to get on their nice, clean overalls. They always started the week with a clean overall.

'The Oliver biscuits would come out from the oven, the small Oliver biscuits, and they were put in big baskets at the end of the table. We were each given a little pile by the side of our big bowl of chocolate. They were very hot, they would burn your fingers, and you would drop the biscuit into the chocolate. It was in a little galvanised bowl. Then you would catch hold of the biscuit and you had a brush, like a paintbrush. You would brush off the chocolate that was covering the biscuit till it was just a light covering back and front. Then you put the biscuit on to greaseproof on your right-hand side – you worked left to right – and so you had, say, ten across the greaseproof and you filled up your sheet of greaseproof. Then you put another sheet of greaseproof on the top, and you kept doing this until it was all finished. They were stacked and they got taken away. And then you didn't have anything else to do with them.

Outside of menu card celebrating the opening of the new Bath Oliver factory in 1900.

Inside of menu card.

That was called single dipping.

'This was always on a Monday morning. We never did them any other time. And then they would stand packed until they went to the actual dipper. She was more qualified, she knew how much she had to leave on the biscuit. She did nothing else bar that. One Monday morning's work by the other girls was enough to keep her going all the week. When she'd got the right covering of chocolate on the biscuits, she made a little pattern across them with a fork. It was like a toasting fork – a wire type of thing – and she'd run that across and you'd have three marks across there. I expect they still do the marks like that.'

So what was happening in the little room in the Fifties was an experiment to see if it was possible to do away with the first Monday morning stage, by dipping the biscuits straight into the chocolate without giving them their first brushing. It seems to have caused problems and one feels for the poor girl, watching the wretched chocolate going white.

This was obviously a business that commanded great loyalty from the people who worked there. To be there when it died was a miserable affair.

'I was the last one to leave in 1961. It was very sad, it really was. They had us in and told us what was happening, and we had to go. My friend and I, we were very upset. They just said it doesn't pay, that's all I can remember.

'I thought it was working. You couldn't understand it when all of a sudden they said there was a rumour going round they were going to close it down. I thought everything was fine. It was a terrible shock. I loved it down there. I think probably what it was, it was just the three of us at first. They did move us in the end, I went right up on the top floor, in a tiny little corner, and I had all these racks round me. I had to be more near where the girls were preparing the cakes, so they didn't have so far to bring it to me. I was very happy there.

'You could buy cakes cheap. I can remember that if there was a damaged cake, I used to say, "A couple of pence, Lil, can I have this cake?", and she was very, very good.'

And that, for a very large number of people, is the kind of thing that makes a firm pleasant to work for, a place where you want to stay. But what an enormous difference there is between Margaret Walters' behind-the-scenes account of the chocolate Olivers and the advertisers' handling of the same theme.

'Like everything from Fortt's of Bath, the chocolate is of very superior quality and blends perfectly with the delicate malten flavour of the biscuits.'

'Chocolate Oliver biscuits comprise the Original Oliver biscuit, daintily coated on both sides with delicious chocolate.'

The industrial penny always has two sides to it and the historian needs both.

Chapter Seven   *The post*

At one time it was considered a great privilege to be a postman. The postman had a secure, respectable job and an established place in the community. Everybody knew him and needed him. He rarely moved from one area to another and he saw his job, sorting and delivering letters and parcels, as one for life. The thought of striking would have been inconceivable and the long, awkward hours were accepted as inevitable. Until recently, there was no shortage of postmen. The pay was not exactly generous, but it was regarded as reasonably adequate and, in any case, there were far worse ways of earning a living, especially working in a factory. A postman's work, inside and outside the sorting office, was not too arduous and it contained a certain amount of variety. One was not forced to fit oneself into the pace of a machine and the rhythm of one's tasks changed over the day. A postman might find the walking and the heavy bag a bit too much for him as he approached retiring age, but reckoned to reach the age of 65 in pretty good health and he usually lived for quite a few years after that. There are a lot of very aged ex-postmen around, men with every appearance of still enjoying life.

And then, gradually, it all began to change. Other kinds of worker discovered the attractions of the five-day week, the night-time, the early morning and weekends received the strange name of 'unsocial hours', social security prevented unemployment from being the disaster it was in pre-war days, and walking even the shortest distance was regarded as either a punishment or a form of social degradation. A new definition of the lower orders was created. They were people who walked.

So postmen in mid-career left the service and young men found working as builders' labourers, and so on, more suited to their taste and temperament. During the Sixties the Post Office found itself desperately short of staff and Her Majesty's Mails took longer and longer to deliver, especially after that most wonderful of all excuses for delay was invented, the idiocy of Second Class Mail. Sunday collections were abolished, because work on a Sunday was called Unsocial Hours; Post Offices opened later and shut earlier; and the reputation and efficiency of the postal services sank to such a low level that the Government threatened to break the Post Office monopoly and allow private enterprise to undertake a delivery system.

Men who spent all their working years with the Post Office and have now retired talk very freely and often bitterly about this. They feel that, for whatever reasons, *their* Post Office has gone downhill and that the postman no longer has the prestige he once had. They will pour all this out in conversation and, if one tries to summarise what they feel and say about the postmen yesterday and today, it amounts to this. It is not easy at the moment for a postman to keep his head high and his tail up. Society has downgraded him from his once proud position and, not unnaturally, he feels miserable and déclassé. This expresses itself in the way he dresses. At one time, British postmen were models of neatness and tidiness. They wore their uniform with pride, and they took great care always to appear well turned out. Nowadays – and retired postmen say this with immense regret – a high proportion of the postmen one sees, especially in the larger cities, are distinctly scruffy and their appearance is no credit to Her Majesty's Postal Service at all.

Victor Rosenburg joined the Post Office as a boy messenger in 1912. He went into the Army in 1914 and when he was demobilised in 1919 he returned to the Post Office as a Sorting Clerk and Telegraphist. It was a time when postal employees were moved about from job to job on a rota. One month they might be working as counter clerks and the next in the sorting office. They could also, in some towns, be required to do jobs on both the postal and telegraphic sides of the business. But it was all very carefully organised, with the division of functions and the hierarchy clearly reflected in the uniforms the men wore, not at all unlike an army.

The uniforms were regarded as very important and the regulations were strict. This is how Victor Rosenburg remembers the situation in what he is sure really were the good old days.

'There were several classes of Post Office employees wearing official uniforms. The outdoor staff predominated. These were Inspectors of Postmen and Boy Messengers, the Postmen and the Mail Porters at the Station Sorting Office, the Boy Messengers and the SC and Ts – the Sorting Clerks and Telegraphists – also at the Sorting Office.

'The six Inspectors controlled the Postmen and Boy Messengers. They wore a dark navy blue uniform of jacket and trousers, with a white shirt and black tie or bow. The jacket was lined with black braid about $\frac{3}{4}$ inch wide, and a similar strip of braid ran down the outside trouser leg. Black buttons were used on the jacket, with a brass GPO sign on the lapels. A round pill box cap was also issued, but the Inspectors rarely wore them.

'Postmen wore dark blue uniform – jacket, trousers, a peaked cap, rather oval shaped, or a shako which was similar to the peak cap, except that it had an extra peak at the back which kept rain off the back of the neck. The collar, lapels and the front edges of the jacket were lined with red piping, and similar red piping ran down the outer seam of each trouser leg. Brass buttons were worn on the jacket and white shirts and black ties were compulsory. A cash allowance was made to Postmen for boots, but all boots worn on duty had to conform to an agreed black pattern. Gold stripes, braid, about 2 inches long and $\frac{1}{8}$ inch wide, were awarded to Postmen for each five years of appointed service (without crime!). These were worn on the breast of the uniform jacket. Most Postmen were proud of their uniform. They enjoyed keeping themselves spick and span, and they liked being recognised by the public as an important part of city life.

'A number of Postmen worked as Mail Porters at the Sorting Office. These men wore the normal dark blue uniform but the cap issued to them was the Army flat top type. It had a gold-coloured band of braid round it, as a distinguishing mark of their status and duties. A small number of Postmen were issued with blue riding breeches and blue puttees. These men were mainly engaged on rural duties. They had a red painted bicycle with a front carrier for the mail bag. Boy Messengers were fitted out well in dark blue. A pill box cap with a strong polished peak, a tunic with a closed collar, brass buttons, trousers, all with red piping, and a pair of strong black boots, were issued twice a year. Black leather belts and pouches were worn by all Boy Messengers. Most boys appeared at work with buttons shining, boots well polished, hair short and faces scrubbed. They and their red-coloured bicycles were a common sight in city life.

'A green, Norfolk-style uniform jacket was issued to the SC and Ts at the Sorting Office, but the public didn't often see this.'

Fresh from the Army, Mr Rosenburg took up his new duties at Bath Sorting Office. It was a busy place, with a lot of men working there. A Victorian building, it dealt with parcels in the basement and letters on the ground floor, with a mess-room on the floor above that. Once or twice a year, the river used to rise over its banks and flood the basement and after more than half a century of that, the Post Office very sensibly decided to move up the road on to slightly higher ground. That was in 1935.

Throughout the Twenties and Thirties, in one building or another, these were the staffing arrangements:

'In the Sorting Office there would be 70 to 80 clerks, sorters.

There was a Superintendent, three Assistant Superintendents and about ten overseers. They were called the Indoor Force. In addition, of course, there were the Mail Porters. They were postmen, who hauled the mail by truck to the railway station and back. They were called Mail Porters. And then there were four men called Stampers, who put the letters through the machines to stamp them. Then there were the Packers. The whole staff was probably in the region of 110 or 120, covering the day and night shifts.'

Once someone joined the Post Office, he usually stayed there for the rest of his working life. 'Once a Post Office man, always a Post Office man.' It was a safe job and the money, for those days, was well above the working-class average.

'When I came back from the Army, in 1919, my first week's wages was £2 17s. 6d. I was then twenty-two years of age, and right through to 1935 it was never more than £4. But when you remember that at the end of the First World War a policeman's pay was only about 28s. a week, and people don't realise how low pay was then. But we managed. I think we were much wiser then in the use of money. We knew our limitations, we didn't expect the earth.'

Prices, of course, were in step with wages and salaries. When Victor Rosenburg bought the house he still lives in, he paid £500 for it, a well-built house, 'with solid walls'.

Nowadays – and this, of course, is at the root of most of the labour problems facing the Post Office at the moment – Post Office employees receive a good deal less than the national average, a fact which has certainly led to a decline in morale. The job, too, is much less varied than it was before the Second World War. People work either in the Sorting Office, or in the

Former main sorting office, Bath. Working from this building in the early 1920s, when Victor Rosenburg was in the early days of his career, were 71 Sorting Clerks and Telegraphists, 129 Postmen and 3 Auxiliary Postmen, with the appropriate complement of Superintendents, Assistant Superintendents, Overseers, Inspectors and Assistant Inspectors. If the Post Office had any shortcomings in those days, it was not for want of supervision.

The letter sorting office as it was in 1975, in use as a book-binders and with the original Post Office tables still fully serviceable.

Head Post Office, with no opportunity to move from one to the other.

Formerly, things were different.

'We took turns in the Head Post Office, at the counter, as counter clerks, so that in the Twenties and Thirties we worked in sections, and each section contained four weeks' nights and four weeks' days. On the four weeks of days, two weeks was on the counter, so we kept in touch, two weeks out of every eight on the counter. The Sorting Office was more muscular work than on the counter. The counter kept you in trim mentally, because all sorts of funny things happened there.

'After the last war, in 1945, they divided the staff. The Sorting Office ceased to be the home of the sorting clerks and became the home of the Postmen, Higher Grade. There is now no connection except in a very small way between the Outdoor Force, the Sorting Office, and the Indoor Force at the Head Post Office, the counter.'

Mr Rosenburg didn't object at all to working at nights or at weekends. This, one has to remember, was before the phrase 'unsocial hours' had been invented.

'I'm sure – and this may be against all medical beliefs – that because we did night work for a month at a time (not one week at a time, a month), we got used to it, and I'm sure it prolonged my life. I'm sure of that. I knew all our chaps there, and we all did night work, no trouble with our digestion or our natural works, and we enjoyed the days off, came to work next night. The only meal you missed really was breakfast. If you came home at three in the morning then you'd sleep until midday, so instead of having breakfast, midday meal and tea, on night work you'd have midday meal, tea and supper. We had supper in a dining hall in the Sorting Office, upstairs.'

There was a cook attached to the dining hall.

'She was called a cleaner, not a cook. I'll tell you why. You see, cleaners were borne by the staff, paid for by the Post Office. Now, the meals were run by the Post Office Refreshment Committee. In order that we should have a cook, and not pay for it, we had a cleaner on the Post Office books who didn't clean, but acted as a cook, so we were getting our cook for nothing. And also, of course, they provided the gas free, so in a sense, Mrs Kite (she nursed me as a child), she used to do the cooking, and you'd take in some bread perhaps some nights, a bit of bacon and egg, she'd do it for you.'

'Everybody in the Sorting Office played chess. You used to see them at night, 11.45–12.15, there would be their sandwiches there, and they'd be pushing a pawn up, you see, all the way down, and very often you'd forget you had to be downstairs by quarter past twelve, when the down mail came in. But we got on very well. There was a very good spirit too, you know.'

At one end of the letter sorting room there was what the men called 'the sneak gallery', a sort of spy box. It had glass walls, so that the overseer could keep an eye on 'crimes', which meant mainly taking registered letters or money out of envelopes. There was very little of this – the risks were too great – but it did happen occasionally. The Post Office had to be quite sure of the facts and this aspect of what was bound to be an unpleasant affair was looked after by the Post Office's own detective organisation, the Investigation Branch. Arrests were never made inside the building. The culprit had to have actually removed property from Post Office premises before an offence had been legally committed.

This, slightly edited to remove any clue to the identity of the person concerned, is how it used to happen.

'He got outside and there were two or three men there from the Investigation Branch. They seized him and he collapsed, but before he collapsed he put his hand into his pocket and tried to stuff these notes into his mouth, to eat them, you see. And he collapsed on the floor. And they said, "Come on, (this is all hearsay now) stand up, be a man." They got him up and they got this packet, because he could never swallow it – there weren't many notes, three or four – and they took him across the floor of the Sorting Office (I saw it), and into what we used to call the Superintendent's room. From there, they phoned his wife up, of course, and eventually he went to prison for six months. The last thing I heard was in the late Twenties, and he'd opened a wireless shop and was doing very well.'

In those days, men were very rarely off work. Victor Rosenburg thinks the Welfare State has made us soft and, in his opinion, the general standard of behaviour was far higher when he was a young man.

'Men went to work when they were half dead. It was their duty to go to work. You would meet men who sat down, saying "I can't stand it any longer", but by then they'd been there five or six hours. The only time a man was off work was perhaps for an operation, that type of thing. I myself was away for two months one time for an operation. But in general we were toughened. Once our system got used to having meals at odd times, we slept well, and we kept well. I know this sounds daft, but in my view the young chaps of those days were far more healthy than they are now, because they seemed to master the inequalities of life. Most of us had been in the Army, you see. We went away boys and came back men. But, if we were ill, we had a Post Office doctor – this was before the days of the

The first motor mail van arrives at Bath Sorting Office, 1920. The time is 5.15 a.m. and two boys with pillow-cases full of stale buns and bread from Fortt's bakery next door are standing in the foreground. The van had solid-tyred wheels, acetylene lamps and no windscreen.

Welfare State – to whom we could go. In my time, first of all it was a Dr Cook in Queen's Parade. Then a chap came to Bath and he stuck up a plate on a door in Sydney Place. Normally they can't do that, you see, they've got to buy a practice. He just stuck up a plate, and the following year the Post Office doctor decided to retire. They get a capitation fee, you see, 1s. 6d. for everybody a year, for each person. So this doctor, he was a Scot, got it. He never looked back, a very clever fellow. You didn't need a certificate, you just went to see him in Sydney Place. But you never would go and see him in those days unless you'd got something really the matter with you.

'I hate to say this, but I think the standard of morality was much higher than it is now. I'm an old man, but I don't feel an old man. One of my chief regrets in life is the standard of behaviour today. I'll give you a case in point. In the summer we ran a cricket side, in the Twenties, the night staff. We'd go and play cricket in Bristol or Bath. If we had to go away to Bristol we had to be on duty at 7.30 at night for the evening shift. If you didn't get back on time, all the chaps on day work who were due off at 7.30 would stay on voluntarily and work and cover us until we got back. If we were an hour late they never asked for any payment for it. We would do the same for them if they were in the same position. Now, I can't imagine people doing that today.'

'I'll give you another example to show you the difference between the workers of the Twenties and today. In the Twenties the night mail from the west of England, Penzance, would reach Bath at ten past one in the morning. This would be brought to the Bath Sorting Office across the road, re-sorted for mail for Dorset, on the old Somerset and Dorset Railway, which left at two forty-five.

'If the mail was ever late – occasionally it was – it would be very difficult to make the connection. So if the mail hadn't arrived at the office by quarter to two, almost every man in the Sorting Office would leave his sorting frame when the train was signalled, dash across the road to the railway station, pick up a bag of mail and run back to the Sorting Office, where it would be opened and everyone would sort it straight away. Normally you had to sort your own mailbag, you see. So you got these men, twenty or thirty men, and in order to make the connection, they'd rush over to the station, pick up a bag, bring it back, open it up and sort it so it was guaranteed to catch the mail at two forty-five on the Somerset and Dorset. Now, I can't see that happening today.'

And, alas, there can be very little doubt that Mr Rosenburg is right. That kind of pride in the job has almost disappeared, at least from large organisations like the Post Office.

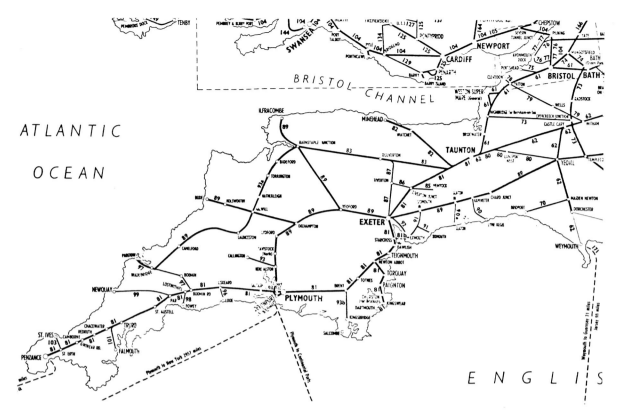

The South-Western railway world of the postman in the Twenties and Thirties.

William Young began work with the Post Office in the mid-Twenties, when he was fourteen. He needed the job badly. His mother had died soon after he was born and his father when he was ten. He was then looked after by an older married brother, who lived in Bridgwater.

'My first job was as an errand boy in a drapery shop in Bridgwater. I was there for six months, November 1924 up to May 1925. I applied to become a messenger and I got an interview. There were two of us for the interview. The other boy was bigger than me, stronger looking, and he got the job. In those days they used to give you the job temporarily and you had your medical afterwards. Fortunately for me, unfortunately for him, he failed the medical – his hearing wasn't up to standard. So they wrote to me and said, "Would you please come and start".'

The letter also said that 'I would be taken on on the understanding that I had my teeth seen to at my own expense', which was no small matter for a boy earning the kind of wage he was getting.

He began his new job with one big disadvantage.

'I couldn't ride a bicycle, so, for the time being, I used to take what they called the near-ones, just round the town, walking. The postmen took me out in the yard and taught me to ride a

William Young as a Post Office Messenger in Bridgwater, 1925. An amateur snapshot, taken with the camera that happened to be available at the time. Fifty-five years later, Mr Young, not surprisingly, cannot remember who took it, or why.

bicycle. Then I could take my full whack of the telegrams, wherever they were for. We used to go anything from four to six miles from the town.

'The office used to be open till about 7 at night. I remember one dark night at the last minute we had a telegram come in for Aswell Hall, which is at Goathurst, about four or five miles from Bridgwater and a hell of a long drive up to the house. I wasn't very old and I honestly felt a little bit scared – it was only oil lamps in those days, mind – so I called round on one of my old school friends and got him to come up with me.'

There were two shifts for the messenger boys, 8 in the morning until 4 in the afternoon, and 12 noon until 7 or 8 in the evening, according to the way the telegrams had been coming in. For this, William Young received 11s. 10d. a week, which was a big improvement on the 7s. he had been earning as an errand boy. 'I thought', he said, 'I was in clover'.

The uniform was strong and solid and there was a certain elegance about it.

'There was a short coat, a reefer coat, and underneath you had a jacket with brass buttons, which meant that you looked smarter in the summer than you did in the winter. There was a one-peak cap. We wore boots; they were provided. You had one uniform at a time, and a spare pair of trousers.'

For a few months after William Young joined the Post Office, however, his legs were covered with breeches and puttees, not trousers. The puttees were a little troublesome to put on, he remembers, and he had to have help from friends and relatives who had been in the Army. The replacement of breeches and puttees by trousers made the messenger boys look rather less military

The telegrams were carried in a leather pouch fixed to the messenger's belt. To keep the messengers dry in wet weather, there was a waterproof cape.

Every day, before beginning work, the messengers had to present themselves and their bicycles for inspection. It was then a question of 'What about that bit of dust on that spoke there?' and 'Your buttons want shining'. The boys' hands and nails were looked at and criticised with the same close attention. Their hair, too, had to be neatly trimmed.

As a Messenger, William Young was required by the Post Office to attend evening classes.

Somerset County Council.

THE COUNTY EDUCATION COMMITTEE.

EVENING CONTINUATION SCHOOLS.

This is to Certify that *William Young*

of *Bridgwater* attended with great regularity at the

Evening Continuation School at *Bridgwater (Eastover)*

during the Session 1926-1927 and received instruction in *Business*
Arithmetic, Geography, Drawing.

J. Burkinshaw

County Education Secretary.

Date *11th April 1927*

In 1926, during the General Strike, the notorious Geddes Axe fell, cutting the wages and salaries of a wide range of public servants. William Young lost a shilling a week, out of his 11s. 10d. 'I don't think they'd stand for that today', he reflected, and of that there can be no doubt whatever. But times were hard and, if you had a safe job, you held on to it, despite wage cuts. And, when he was eighteen, William Young moved on to become a postman. This meant leaving Bridgwater and going into lodgings in the little town of Langport, fifteen miles away, where the postal staff consisted of half-a-dozen men.

'In those days, when you became a postman, they almost inevitably sent you away from home, so that you had to live in lodgings. They didn't send me very far. I went to Langport and took up a postman's duties there. The people I lived with were very nice people. He was a postman. My wages were 28s. 6d. a week, and of that I had to pay 22s. a week lodgings. That was late in 1929. At Langport I used to start at 5.30 in the morning and finish soon after 8. I had a small round. So I had all the morning free until 2 o'clock. Then I went on again till 7 in the evening, and I was cycling all the time. There was no van at all at that time in Langport.'

Those were the days when Langport still had a railway station. Some of the mail came and went that way, but the bulk was transferred in the Post Office van that travelled between Taunton and Yeovil.

The Langport postmen could reckon on very little in the way of perks to supplement their income, but one regular extra was greatly appreciated.

'The doctor's surgery was opposite the Post Office at the bottom of Langport hill. If you took out a bottle of medicine for somebody on your round, you got 1½d. for each bottle or box of pills you took, before you went out. You had to go over and see if there were any for your round, and you used to hope and pray there would be, because those few coppers came in very handy. It was done quite officially, between the local Postmaster and the doctors.'

A year after William Young arrived in Langport, the old bicycle life came to an end.

'Suddenly one day the local Postmaster at Langport said, 'Now, they're going to motorise this area from Taunton, and some of you will have to transfer'. I could have gone to Yeovil, or I could have come to Taunton. As it happened, one of the older postmen at Langport had already served a short term at Taunton, and he said, 'Why don't you come to Taunton, Bill? I could get you fixed up with lodgings, and of course, if you wanted to get home for weekends, Taunton is nearer to Bridgwater than Yeovil is.' So that's how I landed up in Taunton'.

But first there was an important preliminary matter to be dealt with.

'They'd had a message from Taunton to say that I had to be trained on a motorbike and sidecar before I went to Taunton. I had a proper bloke who came over from Taunton and showed me how to go about it and we used to ride all round Somerton, and then for a couple of days we had to go to Taunton on this motorbike and sidecar, and go round all the routes that I'd be covering when I got to Taunton, which happened to be Bradford-on-Tone, Hele, and that part.'

There was no general driving test in those days, but the Post Office had a test of their own. It was not, one gathers, too difficult to pass, and in any case, the roads were fairly empty, especially in the rural areas. So, with his test safely behind him, William Young left Langport for the county town, the motorbike and sidecar and the narrow lanes.

'I travelled to Taunton on the train with my trunk – I've still got it upstairs now. I got to my lodgings in Cleveland Street, found they were alright, and reported to the Post Office at half-past one. I saw the Head Postman, as he was called in those

The Post Office fleet in Taunton in the early Thirties. William Young, in the khaki overall-coat, is standing in the centre of the picture. On the right are, in the trilby, Mr Matthews, Assistant Head Postmaster; next to him, wearing the bowler hat, Mr Haines, Assistant Superintendent; and, hatless and with his hand on the mudguard, Mr Farley, the Mechanic-in-Charge.

days, and he said, "Have you got your motorbike?" I said, "No". Nobody'd told me I had to go to the garage and get my motorbike, but I went down there and got it – it was a BSA – and managed fairly well, although I hadn't been on a motorbike for about a month before that.

'I started off, and I had to drop some mail at Staplegrove. At that time, I was still wearing my old shako, and on a motorbike they weren't much good. It was a fairly windy day, and on the way to Staplegrove my hat had blown off once. At Staplegrove, Mrs Coombes, who kept the Post Office, said, "Aha, a new young man". They used to make you welcome in those days. She said, "How are you getting on?", and I said, "All right, apart from my hat blowing off". "Well," she said, "if you can spare a few minutes, I'll put a couple of buttons on the sides and a bit of elastic", and she did, and I had no more trouble with it. I had to drop some mail at Bishop's Hill and then down to Upcott, and along to Bradford. The Postmistress there, she said, "You're in very good time", and I said, "Well, there's one or two items here that I don't seem to have got rid of", and it transpired that I'd missed out all of Rumwell. I'd bypassed it. Anyway, she was a very sympathetic sort of woman, and she telephoned the Head Postman and said, 'Tisn't fair, you know. This chap's only been round a couple of times and he's done very well, but he's missed out Rumwell. I think you ought to

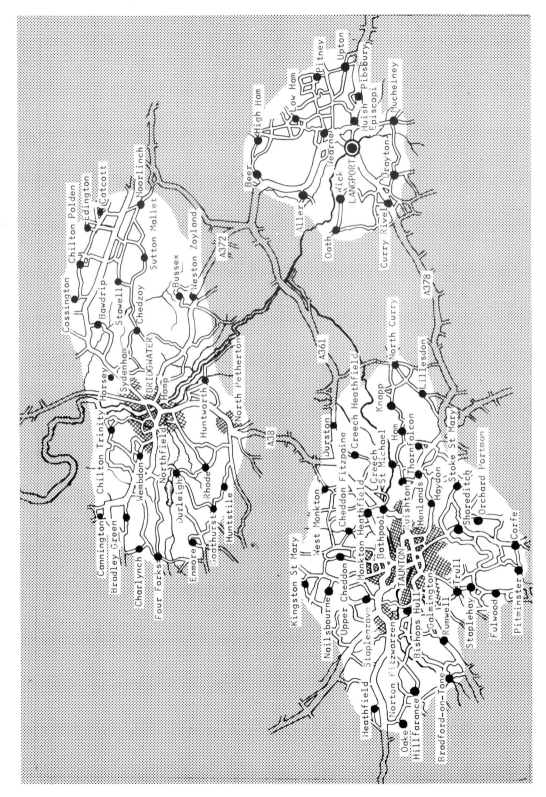

A Somerset postman in the Twenties and Thirties. The map shows typical postmens' 'rounds' of the villages surrounding Bridgwater, Taunton and Langport.

122

The next generation. The Taunton Post Office Annual Dinner, Deller's Restaurant, 1952. Mr William Young is in the centre of the first table, facing the camera. Next to him is his wife and on her left, his son, Bob who had recently joined the Post Office, as a Messenger.

The Head Postmaster, Mr Cutcliffe, is the tall man standing with his back to the window in the centre of the picture. 'He was a disciplinarian, but at the same time he was very fair'.

send somebody out to show him the way round Rumwell and delivery on the way back." So that's what they did.'

And, having dealt with Bradford-on-Tone, Hele, Rumwell and the rest, Mr Young spent the evening collecting the mail in Taunton itself. He usually reckoned to finish about 10.

The sidecars were still being used up till the outbreak of war in 1939, but a year or two before that time arrived, William Young had moved on to vans, doing mainly town work. The vans were Fords and, once again, the driving instruction was thorough, and at the public expense.

And then came the war and, for William Young, whose whole life until then had revolved round Bridgwater, Langport and Taunton, four years as an anti-aircraft gunner on merchant ships, with unpleasant trips backwards and forwards across the Atlantic and into the Mediterranean. He came back safe and sound to Taunton and the Post Office, and rose to the rank of Inspector. In due course, both his sons went into the Post Office too, starting exactly as he had done himself, as messenger boys.

In retirement, he says, with absolute conviction, 'I'm better off now than I've ever been', and, as a commentary on the social changes of the past century, that can hardly be beaten.

Chapter Eight Newspapers and magazines

A large provincial paper has anything between one and two thousand people working for it, while in the case of a major national, such as the *Daily Express* or the *Financial Times* the figure can rise to five or six thousand. Of each thousand employees, about a third will be working on the editorial side, gathering the news, writing it up and preparing the results for the printer; a third will be technical staff of one kind and another; and a third will be involved in getting advertisements, in distributing and selling the paper, and in the accounts and personnel departments. All of these people, no matter what the size of the paper, have had to adapt themselves to great changes in technology and organisation during the past fifty years; in the next half century, if newspapers are to survive at all, these changes are certain to be even more radical and far-reaching.

An inevitable feature of this continuous process of transformation has been the disappearance of many newspapers – two-thirds of the 1920 total are no longer published – and a great deal of unemployment, both temporary and long-term, among the many kinds of specialists who come under the blanket title of 'newspaper men'. Mergers, the creation of new patterns of ownership and publication, and new management styles have, in many instances, destroyed old-established traditions and loyalties and produced a situation in which yesterday's very real corporate feeling, which was taken for granted in the Twenties and Thirties, has to a great extent disappeared from the newspaper world, especially among the younger members of the staff.

Against this background, it is interesting to explore the careers and attitudes of a few people who spent all their working life with newspapers and who have recently retired. The first three are all veterans of the Birmingham-based complex of morning, evening, weekly and Sunday papers, headed by the morning daily, the *Birmingham Post*, and the evening paper, the *Birmingham Mail*. The *Post*, called, to begin with, the *Birmingham Daily Post*, was established in 1857, the *Mail* in 1870. On the occasion of the *Post*'s centenary, the owners, the Birmingham Post and Mail Ltd, published a commemorative history of the paper.[1] In his introductory chapter, the author, H. R. G. Whates, wrote the following:

'In trying to recover and reconstruct the past of the *Birmingham Post* one is reminded of Lord Burnham's remark in doing a similar task for his famous paper. "The *Daily Telegraph*," Lord Burnham writes, "made history but certainly it left none." He had to work on only "casual references in books by members of the staff, a few scrappy memoranda and letters, a fairly reliable memory, and the files of the newspaper itself". There are no books written by members of the *Birmingham Post* staff that throw any light on the paper; letters and memoranda have gone the way of all scrap; living memories do not reach much beyond the paper's Jubilee in 1907. There are indeed the files, over 30,000 daily papers, but they tell very little about themselves. The personal and business reticence of the proprietors, and the journalistic tradition of anonymity, combine in an objectivity more admirable in theory than helpful to a newspaper historian.'

Whates was writing within the conventions of his period, at a time when historians relied almost entirely on source material which had been preserved on paper and which consequently reflected the views and attitudes of the people who habitually used the written and printed word in the course of their work, the record-creating stratum. What is preserved in this form inevitably and invariably represents the point of view of management. The thoughts, memories and experiences of the NCOs and privates of the industrial and commercial army are rarely represented, except accidentally and at second and third hand. They have not found their way on to paper and they have consequently been disregarded, except when the report of a Royal Commission is appointed to investigate this or that scandal or disaster gives the ordinary workers a temporary voice.

For this reason, library-based history can hardly avoid giving a very partial view of what took place in the past. The tape-recorder, still in its clumsy, bulky infancy when Whates was gathering the material for his history of the *Birmingham Post*, has made it both possible and easy to accumulate evidence of an altogether different kind. People can be given the opportunity to say the things they have never had the time, the inclination or the encouragement to write down. And history looks very different through their eyes, so different and, let it be

---

[1] *The Birmingham Post, 1857–1957*, pp. 3–4.

said, so much more interesting and credible, that one shudders to think how much nonsense must have been written in the name of history in ages when documents were accepted at their face value and when no disturbing and heretical facts were permitted to reach the surface from below. The new marriage of library and tape-recorder, of words and pictures, is producing a different kind of history and a different brand of scholarship. Once the historian had begun to see himself as an investigative journalist as well as an analyst, an expert who was as much at home with the living as with the dead, the foundations on which history is built were changed and strengthened. What the tape-recorder has done, in fact, is to allow ordinary people to make a bigger and fairer contribution to history.

Mr K. W. J. Davis went to work at the *Birmingham Post* in 1928 as an office boy when he was fourteen. He got the job largely on the recommendation of Dr Richard Wassall, the organist and choirmaster of St Martin's Church, the Parish Church of Birmingham. Dr Wassall was a considerable figure in the life of the city. In addition to his duties at St Martin's, he was conductor of the City of Birmingham's Police Male Voice Choir, which had a great reputation in the musical field. Mr Davis was a chorister at St Martin's for several years and the *Post* took him on because Dr Wassall said he was a good lad.

'I served in the front office, mainly on the front counter. One of the things I had to do was sort the replies to advertisements into the various pigeon-holes. You sorted the letters into them as rapidly as you could, because they mounted up so quickly. You became almost overwhelmed by them and you were glad when someone said, "Fetch me so-and-so", and you could have a bit of a break from the letters.

'You'd start off the day at eight with two mail bags full and then there were the ones from the advertisement reply boxes which were outside, let into the walls – four of these. After a while other boys would come in and take over the duties and you'd be running round doing other things. At nine o'clock in the morning you'd have to go up into one of the upper offices. This was in the older building, and the then General Manager, a very military gentleman, Major Ford, would sit at the head of the table, and two other persons – secretaries or the Secretary of the Company and others, according to the time of the day or what their business was – would be seated alongside or facing, and I would stand by the General Manager with a paperknife and open the letters and pass them to him. He would then open each one and see what it was. If it was a cheque or something else that fell into a definite category, he would pass it down to the right person to deal with it. And woe betide you if the paperknife went too deep and you cut whatever it was inside it

The old Birmingham Post and Mail office. 'We was very close. Everybody was very close.'

in half. He did this himself because there were so few administrative top people on that side of the newspaper. The General Manager thought he ought to know exactly what was going on, and he certainly did. So at nine o'clock every morning you were there sharp.'

'When the General Manager was away, perhaps on holiday, the Secretary looked after the letters. He was an accountant and everything mixed up into one. He was just as accurate and meticulous as the gentleman he was relieving, just the same.'

The office boy, in his traditional jack-of-all-trades form, no longer exists in Britain but, until the Second World War, he played an indispensable role in commerce. Being the odd-job person about the place, he necessarily had a wide range of tasks to perform and in this way he got a very good idea of how the business worked. The abolition of the office boy was a backward step, and apart from causing the loss of a useful training post, it worked to the disadvantage of secretaries. Before the

127

128

The new home of the Post and Mail.
*'It's not so happy here as it was down
there in Cannon Street.'*

war, a secretary was nearly always a real secretary, with a
well-defined professional function and status. When she had to
take over many of the chores previously carried out by the
office boy, her status declined. Doing away with the office boy
was not only bad for boys; it worked to the disadvantage of
women, although this was certainly an accidental process, not a
feature of any anti-feminist campaign.

A book about the office boy is long overdue, and it needs to
be researched soon, before the last generation of genuine,
old-time office boys has died off. Meanwhile, however, we
have to content ourselves with the reminiscences of such
veterans as Mr Davis, as tantalising clues to the richness of this
largely unexplored field.

The office boy was on the go all day long, at everyone's beck
and call.

'Perhaps the proprietor, Sir Charles Hyde, might press his
buzzer and you'd have to run up the stairs from the front office,
knock at the door and go in, and say "Good morning, Sir
Charles", and he'd just look at you over the top of his heavy
glasses – he was a dark gentleman, thickset, said very little, a
very nice kind gentleman – and just say, "Fetch my cigarettes
from so-and-so", and give you a £5 note. This £5 note to me
was like a piece of wallpaper, I'd never even seen one before.
You'd come back with the cigarettes. You'd leave that office
and go downstairs again, and the buzzer would go and it would
be the General Manager, Major Ford, and you'd go upstairs and
he'd say, "Come in, wretched boy, do this or do that, make my
fire up". You'd make his fire up. If you dropped a lump of coal
on the grate, because you were shaking, you just got shouted at.
You never came to any harm – he was just that sort of man,
very autocratic. Once or twice I've walked in the door and
someone had irritated him, and he just shouted, "Come in,
wretched boy", you'd walk in, he'd have a pile of correspon-
dence, and he'd just throw it over the room for you to catch.
Naturally you dropped it, and then he used to let fly. It didn't
amount to anything, it was all part of an act, I think, because
basically he was quite a kind chap. If he thought you didn't look
very well, he'd say, "What's the matter with you, Davis, aren't
you getting enough food to eat?" and that sort of thing. So
you'd go downstairs again.'

And that was how fourteen year olds learnt about human
nature and people in authority. It was a rough and ready
training, but it was a good deal more realistic and in touch with
life than most of the courses that teenagers get sent on
nowadays.

But there were compensations. Sir Charles Hyde used to give
garden parties for the staff at his home, "The Moat", at
Bernswill.

129

The Newsroom at the Post and Mail *today. The sound insulation is so good that the three ladies on the balcony can hear nothing whatever of the typewriters, telephones and general bustle down below. Silent journalism has arrived.*

'Artists like Gert and Daisy used to entertain us on these occasions. Sir Charles hired a fleet of buses to take his employees there and back. Many old employees still talk of these garden parties even now. Later on, after Sir Charles died, the Company used to give a dance at the Grand Hotel, Birmingham, on four separate nights. This went on for some years and then the operation became too large and came to an end.'

The *Birmingham Post* was a confusing building:

'A rabbit warren in many ways. Quite an experience, though. When I say rabbit warren, I don't mean it disrespectfully, because a lot of these old Victorian places had arches, doors, stairways, hidden little pokey holes and big, unexpected basements and, being a printing office, it was also a type of factory, with old machines with tunnels underneath. Sometimes we had to run under the tunnels and be careful we didn't get caught on a trolley carrying printing plates along through the narrow tunnel.'

One of the more agreeable aspects of the office boy's job was that it gave one a chance to get outside the building a good deal.

'You had to go to the Post Office twice a day to fetch the mail bags. These were heavy bags and you were little boys. The Post Office in Birmingham was five hundred yards or more away, up busy New Street.

'We used to run all sorts of errands, used to fetch things, used to have to change the towels in the washroom, under the charge of a very irate lady. If you didn't put those towels correctly, or if the soap wasn't there, you'd get a box across the ears. Those were the days when there were very few women or girls working in newspaper offices. At the *Post* there was only one, as far as I can remember, or possibly two in the offices. There might have been a lady artist. There was a lady editor of the then weekly paper, the *Weekly Post*, very knowledgeable, a very nice person, quite old. There was one lady typist for the Secretary and the General Manager, and beyond that I think there were some ladies in the canteen, and that was it.'

The office boy's job was exactly that, a job for a boy. It gave one a foothold in the firm and one kept a close lookout for any opportunity to climb the ladder. Mr Davis was exceptionally lucky.

'I stopped in the front office for roughly six months. I think I did pretty well everything, went everywhere, used to fetch adverts from advertisers, run messages, just a general errand boy. They paid me 7s. 6d. a week. I was glad to get the job, really glad, because there were just not any jobs going.

'Then one day the kindly gentleman who was in charge of the office, Mr Spencer Cross – he was a perfect gentleman, one of the kindest men I think I've ever met – stopped me one day and said, "I wonder if you'd like a change?" He said they wanted a lad in the Wire Room, that was the term then, the Wire Room. I said "yes" straight away, I never even thought into it. I suppose it was a bit impetuous, but the thing that attracted me about this place, the Wire Room, was that they used to have a lot of flashing lights. The circuits were always flashing all the time and it used to fascinate me. So I went. Whether I made the right choice or the wrong choice we'll never know, but I went up there.

'I think I got 12s. 6d. a week then, but I worked just as terribly hard and the hours were very, very awkward. I really worked. The old chap there in charge was an ex-Post Office employee, a dyed-in-the-wool Victorian, and this Victorian attitude permeated the whole of the building. "You've come here to work to earn money to get the crust for the next day. Don't come here to do us a favour. If you come, you work." And that was it, you did just that, and you never thought anything else about it. And you worked correctly and properly, and you really put everything you thought you should into that job. I stayed there, and the rest of my working life was in communications, with the same company.

'It was shift work and the hours were unsocial, to use the present idiom, but it was fascinating and the thing that really made the job for me was the fact that slowly but imperceptibly the apparatus and the systems were changing and developing. There was always something new coming over the horizon. It still is that way. So you weren't in a dead-end job where your brain never got exercised, but you still had to work hard. For a time I didn't do night work, but I did evening work. I used to finish at eight o'clock. We did half a day on Wednesday. It was 48 hours a week, at least. You might start at eight, or ten, or eleven.'

Without knowing it when he said "Yes" to Mr Cross, Mr Davis had come into Press communications at a very interesting time. The Croydon based specialist, Creed and Company, had a virtual monopoly of telecommunications equipment. Before the First World War, Creeds had perfected and marketed what was known as the Creed High Speed Automatic Printing Telegraphy System. This punched and decoded morse messages on tape. At the sending end, there was a tape perforator controlled by compressed air and controlled by a keyboard similar to that of a typewriter. The information recorded in this way was sent over a telegraphic line and, at the receiving end, a reperforator recorded the incoming signals and a printing machine accepted the received message tape and decoded it into plain language printed characters on ordinary paper tape. Potential customers were slow to show an interest in the new equipment, but gradually sales resistance was broken down and in 1912 the *Daily Mail* became the first newspaper in the world to adopt the Creed system. In a very short time, the entire contents of the paper were being transmitted daily from London to Manchester for simultaneous publication. Previously, the copy had had to be decoded and written out by hand in Manchester by a large staff of telegraph clerks.

In the early Twenties, the Press Association began using this type of equipment between London and provincial centres for the newspapers subscribing to their agency service. By modern standards, the machines were clumsy, since a supply of compressed air had to be piped to each machine from a central compressor plant. By 1925, electrically-driven machines eliminated the need for compressed air and it was possible to have page printing, as an alternative to the original tape printing equipment.

The teleprinter arrived from the United States in 1923. This was what was known as a direct printer, recording messages direct from the incoming line, instead of from tape via a reperforator. It was not until after the Second World War that teleprinter working took the place of high-speed Creed-Morse throughout the country.

All subsequent equipment has been a series of more sophisticated and faster machines, based on the principles described above. Telex services, used by newspapers as much as by any

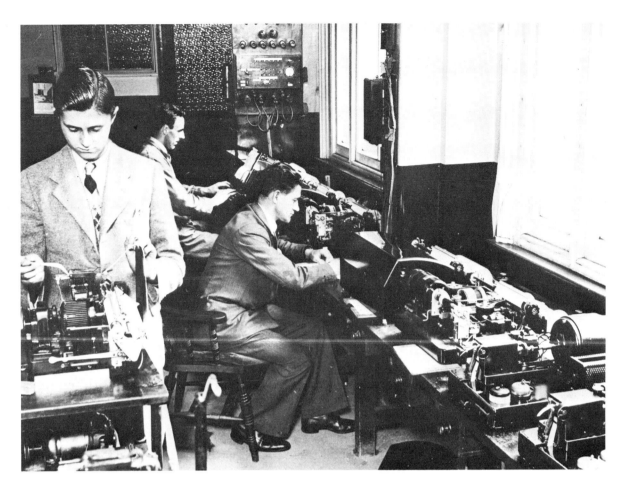

The Post's *Wire Room in the mid-Thirties. Mr K. W. J. Davis, working at his Creed machine, is furthest from the camera.*

other kind of business concern, have developed to a remarkable extent since the end of the Second World War. They are the teleprinter counterpart of the normal subscriber to subscriber telephone service. The expansion of telex and leased private telegraph services has greatly reduced the amount of traffic sent over the public telegraph services from which they sprang. Nowadays, the public telegraph services deal largely with social messages and between business organisations having too low a volume of traffic to justify the rental charges for private equipment.

Picture transmission by wire was not widely used until the Thirties, although as early as 1928 several of the larger newspapers installed transmitters and receivers for the purpose. Before 1939, however, picture apparatus was possessed by very few newspapers, but nowadays there are very few offices of any size which are without a picture receiver, although a higher proportion are without picture transmitters.

Mr Davis lived through all these changes and learnt how to

use the equipment simply by working with it, by trial and error.

'You just learnt as you went, the hard way. Even the repairing of the machines you had to learn the hard way. Sometimes it was a good way, but when the professional mechanics came they used to shudder to see how we'd done it, but they couldn't deny that it worked that way. The only mechanic we had was a linotype mechanic. We'd send for him and he used to come down. The ceremony then was: "Good morning, Mr Turner", "Good Morning, Mr Pickup". "Would you look at this machine for me, please?" And then out would come the snuff box, a pinch of snuff, and then they'd turn round and say, "Out of the way, lad, what's the matter with this?" Trying to keep the machine going, you poured paraffin or something over it. It usually worked, unless there was a part broken, and in that case you went on to a spare machine. That was the system. Then gradually the machines became more sophisticated and there was no latitude for these old ways of repairing them. Finally they brought in a professional mechanic, a resident mechanic who'd worked at Creeds, and was then *au fait* with that type of thing. Towards the end of his working days he in his turn became obsolete in his ideas, although he still went on doing the job. After a time we had purely mechanical and purely technical people, so you got a split maintenance section. Meantime the poor operators had to pick things up as best they could, with different types of apparatus coming in all the time, including telephoto keyboards. We'd never been trained on a keyboard, but we brought keyboards in. We had to learn that, and you had to be good.'

There were no suitable courses that all-rounders like Mr Davis could be sent on, not in Birmingham, anyway.

'There was a night school up in Suffolk Street, but the only course they ran was a technical course for Post Office people. One of the operators said, "You ought to learn a bit more, you know, because things are changing technically", and I said, "I agree on that, but what can I do about it?" Anyway, I went up to Suffolk Street; I became accepted on the Post Office course, which involved telephone exchanges and all sorts of things, nothing to do with my job. It broadened my horizons but it bored me to tears. I had to pay for it myself, and I always went when I finished work and I used to fall fast asleep on the tram going home, really bushwacked. I used to go twice a week up there. I didn't understand half of what they said. The only thing that fascinated me was magnetism and electricity, because the teacher there was a bit of a comedian in his way. He was a character.'

The work was hard, but it was interesting and, by the time

Mr Davis demonstrating modern electronic communications equipment shortly before his retirement.

one was a fully fledged operator on the full Union rate, well paid – over £4 a week.

'It was all Morse code, high speed automatic Morse and manual Morse, and you used to hear these other papers chattering in the sounder or sounders, when we got more circuits in, and you became so interested and you knew a lot of these chaps by the sound. It was like looking into a mirror. One man sending Morse didn't sound like another man sending it, not at all. You could name the man, if you knew him, you could name him. You could tell who it was as though you were looking at his picture. You knew his idiosyncracies, the way he'd send his figure four, or his figure six.'

This is how they learnt their Morse.

'You had a little practice key there, by the side of you, and you just wrote the Morse code down on a piece of paper. The overseer used to come over, show you how to fix your wrist and hold the key properly, and you just went on from there. You just learnt it by sheer hard slogging, nothing else. And then they'd come over and correct you. You did that in your own time when there was no work to do, or you weren't sorting anything, or making the tea, or polishing the machines.'

It was a tough life for a fourteen year old.

'At that time, I lived in Yardley, which was four miles away, and I used to come to work on the tram, but when the hours got a bit difficult I became the proud owner of a bicycle and used to cycle. When you were on shift work and there was no trams or buses, you just used your bicycle, all weathers, fair and foul.

'Very often, I used to bring something for my lunch, but there was a canteen which was very reasonable. It had to be, because your money was so limited. They were kind, the ladies. If they thought you were a little lad, they used to put just a little bit more on the plate. Or if you sat talking to an old-timer, perhaps he was 60-odd and you were a young lad, he was a bit paternal, and he'd say, "Well, would you like a block of chocolate, lad?", something like that, you know.

'But the discipline in the offices was so strict. If the news dried up on all circuits you weren't allowed to read a newspaper or talk. The overseer used to say to me, "If you've got no work to do, find some, make yourself useful." That included sorting hundreds of stock sheets out ready for use by the telegraphist over the wire next day or the same day, mixing the glue, which was a horrible, smelly business. You had to go down into the machine room to a great tub with a bit of a stick and an old metal jug, and you'd ladle the glue up. I was only a shortish lad, and one day I went too far and I became stuck in the glue. I wasn't sympathised with, I was just shouted at for being such a long time getting myself clean afterwards.'

The Wire Room could be something of a madhouse.

'I can remember being on the night shifts and you used to go so tired. They'd send such a huge amount of stuff that nothing could be coped with. After two o'clock in the morning the work became spasmodic and you knew that you were going to go very dozy, the office would quieten down, the Press Association would quieten down. So what we used to do, in the days of the old Morse sounders, was to insert a metal clip between the top and the actual sounder itself, and that seemed to magnify the thing. Then you put it on the loudest reflecting surface you could find and you'd put your head on the table. You never failed to wake up, you never overslept. As soon as the sounder clicked you were awake. I can remember when Hitler invaded the Low Countries and they called us in. It came on the automatic, and we woke up for it.'

There were a lot of air-raids on Birmingham and the paper was often produced under great difficulties.

'When the siren went, we used to have to take some of our telegraphic instruments on a trolley down to the air-raid shelter in the basement. We connected them up to the lines and carried on working. We always waited until the very last moment before moving the stuff down there, so that we could get as much news as possible before transferring ourselves to the basement. One day all our lines went and we had to work from the *Wolverhampton Express and Star* and send our copy back by road.'

After experiences like this, Mr Davis found life in the Army comparatively peaceful. Not surprisingly, he was a communications expert in uniform. After the war, he returned to the *Mail* and finished up as Communications Manager with the paper. Looking back over half a century, he feels that, from a human point of view, things have certainly changed for the worse. He feels this is particularly true in the Composing Room. Half a century ago, 'I used to go through the Composing Room, and they looked that calm, solid type of man, still working very accurately, as though there was more residual strength in them than there is with the chaps today. Nowadays, it seems as if they are under pressure all the time. It's all programmed, there's no hysteria, they're just working very hard, but they've got a tighter schedule to meet now. Although we used to run editions with every race in the old days, there never seemed the panic or the frustrations. Naturally, if you're beating the clock you're always going pretty well at the double, but everything's different today. I think there's more tension and more worry. They try to give a good service, a better service, but if you are being speeded up, there's bound to be the occasional slip. In the old days, the compositor used to sit on a little stool doing the Stock Market reports with tweezers, picking the figures out and popping them into the galley calmly and deliberately. There were never any mistakes.'

His colleague, Mr J. J. Coffey, joined the paper thirty-nine years ago. He began as a floor hand in the machine room, gathering up the waste paper and baling it up and sweeping round the machines. There was a rigid protocol about work in this area of the building. Promotion was as fixed and firm a business as in the police or the services. One did so many years in this rank, and so many in that. There was nothing haphazard about one's progress and no stage could be missed. So one had the prescribed spell as a floor hand.

'Then you automatically became a fly-hand – farrag-hands they call them today. You sat and knocked them up on your knees, stacked each quire. You sat on a little stool. You had that job six, maybe seven years. Every time there was an edition you were on a certain machine, that was your job. You prepared the machine previously in the day. You got a bit of a break between editions, but the hours were from nine to six. You came on the job at nine.

'Then you're qualified as time goes on. You go into the next stage of the job, that's what we called a rail-hand. That's mounting the rails, loading the paper up underneath, on the bottom deck, manhandling it, no modern methods. Then you'd feed it through the machine from your section to the next section above, to the upper grade men. That's when you'd become a rail-hand, as they called them. You've got your floor-hand, when you first start, that's cleaning up, then you've got your farrag-hand, fly-hand we used to call it, and then rail-hand, and from that position through your webs, and wind it through to fold 'em. When that's done you come from your bottom job, come up and help load up, plate up, in other words. You're still on the same job, part of your rail-hand's job is to help load the machine up.'

The ritual continued:

'Next you came to another stage of grade, control-hand, we used to call it in Cannon Street, a brake-hand. He was responsible for stopping the machine. Anybody could start and stop it. You had to go through all these grades before you could finally be the top man on the machine. In the present day and age, there was an agreement so that we could take our men, bring them in the NGA, you see, which years ago wasn't allowed. We were also NATSOPA men. But the man we called the minder – he's called a Machine Manager nowadays – was always NGA. But I stayed NATSOPA all the way through. I finished up NAT-SOPA.'

These are the niceties of Trade Union membership and organisation that mean so much to the men inside the printing trade and so little to people outside, the ritualistic observances, about which people are prepared to argue with all the passion and conviction of a medieval theologian.

Mr Coffey was very fond of the paper's old building in Cannon Street.

'I loved it. We was very close. Everybody was close. You walked down the corridor, you'd meet an office man, or you'd meet a foundry man, you'd meet a publisher. Now, you're all put miles apart from one another and I think, the feeling's general, that's why it's not so happy here as it was down there in Cannon Street. It's still friendly, but you're isolated from one another here. If you see somebody you're friendly enough with them, but you're not mingling in together. In the old place, a person would come through the Machine Room on the way to another office, they'd have to come through the Machine Room.'

There is considerable irony about this. A new building is planned with the greatest of care to be convenient and efficient and comfortable to work in, and it finishes up by being, from a human point of view, far less satisfactory than the old building it has replaced. The problem is a common one and much too little attention has been given to it. The people involved are

The Machine Room. 'You can get through two pairs of overalls a week here. A pair in Cannon Street would last you a fortnight.'

sensitive to the change. Like families shifted from a slum street to a new housing estate or large block of flats, they miss what Mr Coffey calls 'the closeness'. It is 'closeness' which makes a submarine a much happier ship than an aircraft carrier and a small restaurant a more friendly and agreeable place to work than the Ritz, and *The Times* in Old Printing House Square a paper for which its employees were proud to work. In these cramped premises, everybody knows everybody else. Even more important, this unavoidable physical closeness creates a distinctive management style. Mr Coffey put it this way:

'The General Managers and the Editors were all gentlemen, in my opinion. They acknowledged you and spoke to you as an ordinary person. Now they don't, we're too far apart, you see. The building's done that. In Cannon Street, the General Manager would walk through the Machine Room to a department and say, "Hello, Jim. Hello, John." That doesn't happen here. Mr Jack White, the old Foreman, he was 93 when he died and he retired when he was about 85, I think. He stayed because his heart and soul was in the family surroundings. He loved the place. He was an efficient man and he looked upon everyone as his sons. All the chaps, he looked on them as sons, and they looked on him as a father. He'd help us out, if we had a bit of trouble at home. Go and speak to him, and he'd say, "Alright, get off home and see your wife." He'd see our work was covered. That's what I mean by a gentleman.'

Curiously enough, from a purely technical point of view, the old building was in some respects more efficient than the new one.

'We get dirtier here than we did in Cannon Street, and we're in a modern machine room. It just happened. You can get through two pairs of overalls here. A pair in Cannon Street would last you a fortnight. There's so many different methods. There's so much spray here, more spray, you see. We complained, we were always complaining, but what could they do? They had detectors and everything, to try and see if they could steady it up.'

Interesting facts like these are not, perhaps, very likely to appear in the next volume of the official history of the *Birmingham Post* and *Mail* group. But they are typical of the everyday things that people working on the production of these papers are talking about all the time. And they raise the important question, 'What is a newspaper?' Fifty years ago, this would have seemed a ridiculous point to bother one's head about, but nowadays, when the old social order has almost gone and Jack has no doubt at all that he is as good as his master, one is forced to think much harder about definition. And in the process one is likely to make some surprising and maybe disturbing discoveries. If one looks carefully at any history of what is traditionally called 'the Press', one finds oneself reading about a world of editors, proprietors, finance, mergers, closures, circulation figures, technical changes, political pressures and outstanding journalists. One is presented, in other words, with the Press as it appears to those who own and run it.

But this is to concentrate only on the top of the press pyramid, and to ignore the much larger army of technicians, office staff of all kinds, distribution and transport workers who make the appearance of the paper possible. Their morale, skill and loyalty, at any period, are vital. They brood, intrigue, discuss personalities and cherish grievances, exactly as the management do. The only difference lies in the important fact that the far more numerous heartsearchings, successes, failures and arguments of the rank-and-file usually go unrecorded, and the picture one obtains of a business is consequently unbalanced and, not infrequently, untrue.

One of the most prominent and powerful figures in the long history of the *Post* and *Mail* was the General Manager for getting on for half a century, Col. Sir Bertram Ford. Appointed in 1913, he was a man of markedly military tastes and habits, a

140

Col. Sir Bertram Ford, General Manager, The Birmingham Post, *1913–43, Managing Director, 1943–47. 'Come in, wretched boy.'*

fact well known to both his staff and to the numerous people from the outside world who had occasion to meet him. In the official history of the company, he is described in these terms:

'In personal affairs he was fundamentally just and always strictly honourable. He was quite incapable of a mean or dishonest action, his prejudices dissolved at a call to humanity and he would go to any amount of trouble to help a man in difficulties.'[2]

2 Whates, p. 230.

141

This is the language of obituary, not of biography or considered history, and discussions with former employees of the paper make it clear that such glowing praise is, to say the least, not completely in accordance with the facts. One man in particular, with bitter experience of the way in which his sick father, a compositor of twenty years' service, was treated by the General Manager, went so far as to say that the assessment of Sir Bertram just quoted was 'a pack of lies'.

One certainly runs a considerable risk in not consulting the troops when a general's reputation is being weighed and recorded for posterity, and it is wise not to take a paragon's qualities for granted. They should be checked as carefully as one checks any other kind of historical data and the only way of doing this is to meet and talk to the right people. Reading between the lines is an art the reader needs to practise constantly. There are remarkably few paragons able to stand the test of conversations with their subordinates and statements such as this one about Lord Iliffe, who bought the paper in 1943 should certainly bring one's critical instincts into play.

'He was known in Fleet Street as a model employer, who commanded the loyalty and respect of all who had the privilege of working for him.'[3]

To which one is entitled to object, 'How do you know?' 'To whom have you talked?' *Ex cathedra* judgements, unsupported by evidence, are always suspect. What one requires, in order to set one's doubts at rest, is the kind of documentation which begins, 'Jack Thompson, who worked for thirty years in the paper's composing room, told me that wages there were always well above the national average and that, during the three months that he was away from work after an operation, the company continued to allow him £3 a week, although it was under no obligation to do this', and 'We have further tribute of Henry Tewson who, in 1932, was taken on as an office boy, after his father, who was Chief Clerk in the Accounts Department, had been forced to give up work after a heart attack. Unemployment was very bad at the time and plenty of the other boys of Henry's age had great difficulty in finding a job'. With a row of testimonials of this order, one has no difficulty in believing that Lord Iliffe was indeed a model employer, but when such evidence is lacking, one is apt to become cynical. In all company histories there is a marked tendency for chairmen and managing directors to be preserved for posterity as paragons, although conversation with former employees not infrequently brings one to less flattering conclusions.

Any enterprise looks different from the bottom. The boardroom and the shopfloor have their own particular attitudes

[3] *ibid.*, p. 232.

towards the past. They may overlap, but they are never identical. Those who receive orders see life rather differently from those who give them. They usually work in less agreeable surroundings, and they meet a different kind of person, with different prejudices and with access to a different level of information about the business.

The building in which one works is of great importance. Some buildings are friendly and encouraging, others exactly the reverse. Many veteran employees of the *Birmingham Post* and *Birmingham Mail* are very outspoken in their preference for the old congested rabbit warren of a building in New Street, where amenities were minimal. The Accounts Department, for instance, was in what was popularly known as the 'pigeon loft', a converted lavatory. The old building was so small that when one walked along the corridors one constantly bumped into people from all the other departments. Isolation was imposs-ible. In the present bright and spacious premises, on the other hand, one department is effectively cut off from another and the directors are shut off from everybody else. There is conse-quently, in the view of people who knew the *Post* and *Mail* in the old days, far less corporate feeling about the place, fewer people who really care about the paper.

This is especially true, perhaps, on the production side, where union attitudes have hardened since 1945. The concept of a newspaper as a team effort, involving a wide range of people doing their best to get the paper out and into the hands of customers, has largely disappeared, in the view of many old timers. Nowadays, a newspaper building is simply a place in which one earns a living.

One ex-printer, whose family has been connected with the industry for several generations, put it this way. In the Twenties and Thirties, he told us, 'an overseer in the composing room would go up to a man and say, "George, set this up for us. Do this on the line or do this on the mono", and he'd do it. And if he said, "George, they're short of a machine-minder there", he'd go and do a bit of machine minding. Or if they wanted something set by hand, he'd do that, too. But nowadays he'd say it was somebody else's job. The skill and the adaptability have gone out of it. In the old days, a compositor used to be able to look after any aspect of the job. But not now.'

During the past twenty-five years printers in Britain have become well known in the industrial world for their high pay and reluctance to accept changes in technology. The word 'Luddites' is not infrequently hurled at them, and with a great deal of justice. It is worth pointing out, however, that printers, like other kinds of workers, have memories, and they have a deep-rooted and perfectly natural fear of returning to anything like the conditions of the Twenties and Thirties.

Take, for instance, the case of Mr Timberlake, who spent fifty-one years in the printing trade in the London area, beginning as a boy of fourteen on 1st August 1922, and retiring on 1st August 1973. He belonged to a printing family. His father, a foreman compositor, died when he was five, his brother served an apprenticeship as a compositor and it was his own wish to do the same. He was promised an apprenticeship, 'but the son of a friend of a director of the firm naturally had preferment'.

So he got what job he could in the printing field. To begin with, he worked with Eyre and Spottiswood, interleaving brown paper between sheets of coloured print, practising machine-feeding whenever he could. He carried buckets of hot water for the men to wash themselves at midday and when they finished work in the afternoon. They paid him an extra sixpence a week for this.

'There were no washrooms. The lavatory was outside – just a long plank with holes in it. There were partitions along the plank and doors open at the top and bottom. The lavatories were flushed from a pipe every so often, and you had to be alert and jump to safety when it all rushed past you. Eyre and Spottiswood were Bible producers and the scrap paper from the Bibles was used in the lavatories. It was of very high quality.'

This, it should be emphasised, was in the 1920s, not the 1820s. But, thankful to have a job at all at a time when millions were unemployed, he stayed with Eyre and Spottiswood as a machine-feeder until he was twenty-one. He then had to leave, because 'it was the firm's policy to dismiss everyone at twenty-one, so that they "could get wider experience in the trade".' So he turned to newspapers and spent the rest of his working life in this branch of printing – Odhams Press, the *Daily Express*, the *Daily Telegraph*, the *People* – never knowing how long the job was going to last, being at the whim of overseers, having to keep standing all the time and to have a cup of tea while one continued working, since no rest periods were allowed in those days.

The best place he ever worked was at Odhams, in Long Acre. Relations with the management were exceptionally good there. The overseer was first-class – 'the men could do no wrong in his sight in his dealings with other departments' – the wages were good and the work was regular. Each week Mr Timberlake worked five days and one night, which meant that on Fridays he worked for twenty-four hours at a stretch, a thought which few printers today would find attractive.

Mr Timberlake survived more or less unscathed, but others were not so tough or so lucky. Mr K. A. Phillips, for instance, recalls what happened to his own father, a machine-minder on four national newspapers, the *Daily Mirror*, *News of the World*, *Daily Herald* and *Daily Mail*.

'My father,' he says, 'was a political fanatic and gambler. His unsocial working hours, early morning gambling and numerous political meetings made any real contact with my mother impossible. During the Spanish Civil War, his time was even more taken up with politics. He volunteered as an anti-fascist early in the Second World War and this caused the final break-up and divorce. My mother found a reasonable man in his place.

'I feel the printing industry itself caused the problem, as basically he is a very kind, gentle and docile man, as his second marriage and the adoption of four children proved.'

'The printing industry', however, covers a very wide range of publications and working conditions. There are the small firms and the giants, the pleasant family concerns and the impersonal publishing machines, the antique and the modern. Bert Bray spent his whole career within the orbit of a periodical with no exact equivalent anywhere else in the world, the *Illustrated London News*.

Founded in 1842 by a printer, Herbert Ingram, the *Illustrated London News* was the world's first illustrated weekly newspaper. It pioneered one new technique after another, it made a point of employing the best available writers, artists and, eventually, photographers, and it was immensely successful. By 1863 it was selling 310,000 copies a week. In 1900 Bruce Ingram, the grandson of the founder, became editor, at the age of twenty-two, and held the post until his death sixty-three years later.

By the 1930s, the *Illustrated London News* was the centrepiece of eight illustrated papers broadly similar in style. Grouped under the ownership and general control of Illustrated Newspapers Ltd, they included such well-known periodicals as the *Tatler*, *Bystander*, *Sketch* and *Sphere*. Lord Thomson bought the lot in 1965, dismissed the editor, Hugh Ingram, who had been in the job less than two years, and closed down all the papers except the *Illustrated London News*, which was the one he really wanted. It was a massacre, but probably an inevitable massacre. In the 1960s the sales of the paper began to slump, mainly as a result of television, and in 1971 it was completely transformed and published monthly instead of weekly. Its circulation recovered and it is now once again in a prosperous condition.

Bert Bray watched it all happen and survived. He went to work in 1927, when he was fourteen, as a junior clerk with a small, but enterprising firm called the London Electrotype Agency, usually referred to as LEA. LEA was a picture agency, which sold photographs to newspapers and magazines. It worked very closely with the *Illustrated London News* and in time it was absorbed into the Illustrated Newspaper group. Mr Bray worked for LEA at several addresses, all within easy reach of Fleet Street, including 10 St Bride's Avenue (1927–34); 32–34 Fetter Lane (1934–41) until this building was blitzed; and Ingram House, the Illustrated Newspapers building at 195 Strand. He progressed to Senior Clerk, to Assistant Manager and then, finally, Manager, a working life spent wholly with pictures.

During his early years, LEA was run by a man named Buckworth, for whom Bert Bray had the greatest respect, a genius wholly devoted to his work. He was by no means a wealthy man.

'He never took much out of the business at all. In fact, I understand the directors at the time said how silly he was to take so little – I wasn't supposed to know these details, but, as the years go by, things go by, and I found an envelope with these things in them. As far as I know, he never took any more than about £8 or £10 a week out of it. He lived at Streatham and he used to come in every morning before half-past eight and, if we weren't in there then, there'd be a shindig. At a quarter-past five – we had a gas-ring in the office, up on the third floor, and an old zinc sink, next to the toilets – quite a luxury in those days, two toilets, one for the lady, one for the gents – and I used to have to fill up the kettle, put it on the gas-ring, and take the boiling water upstairs for him to have his wash with. And he used to call out, "Bray, where's my water?", if I'd been sent out on another job and hadn't had a minute to breathe, and I'd say, "Just coming, sir".

'And I'd take his water up and he'd have his wash and he'd come down and, if you went past his office, you could see him – he had a mirror on the wall – with his two brushes, brushing his beard down nicely. He wouldn't go home without his hands immaculate, beard immaculate, he'd brush his overcoat, his bowler hat. He would have everything done right.

'He was a wonderful man, really, because he'd started this agency, and it was a very complicated agency, and therefore he had to train his staff. One day the head of another agency – I think it was Fox – rang up and said he wanted to speak to Mr Buckworth and said, "I want to speak to you about that young fellow Bray you've got. Do you want to part with him?" Buckworth said, or words to this effect, "What do you mean?" and the other chap said, "I can offer him a better job down here", and Buckworth said, "How dare you ring me up and ask to take a member of my staff, who I'm training? I don't have staff come here unless they're willing to work for me and to put in a full day's work. And you come to me and ask to take one of my staff."

It was Bert Bray's extreme good fortune to work under two remarkable men, whom he admired and with whom he seems to have got on very well – Mr Buckworth and Sir Bruce Ingram. His memories of Bruce Ingram tell one a lot about the way the paper was run and produced and account, in one way, for the ultimate decline and take-over, since the tradition which this extraordinary editor did much to create eventually became fossilised and a barrier to survival.

'He always gave me the impression that he knew what he

147

wanted – no gossip, no murders. We used to have *True Detective* and all those come on to us, saying, "The *London News* must have used this or that", but we hadn't. Sir Bruce didn't want that publicity for the ILN. He wanted the ILN to go all over the world as a magazine which came from London with the best possible material in it. And he kept it like that. Whether it became old-fashioned is beside the point.

'Bruce Ingram might have been aristocratic in one way, but in the other way everybody respected him. I've known the time when I've gone into the editorial office and another chap could bear me out on this, that was Reg Smith, who was art editor of the *London News* at one time. When they got all the photographs together – say it was going to be a double page on one particular subject – they'd have all these prints done, say there was ten pictures. Bruce's mind would go in such a way that he'd go down on his knees on the floor and say after a while, "Reg, move that one. Top, bottom right, over there, no, not there, there, top left." So Reg would move it into position. What he was working out was impact. When people open a magazine, they look first at the right-hand page, so the best of the pictures were on this side, right side, but they've got to be balanced with those on the left side.

'He had a good eye, a wonderful eye for a picture. And all of a sudden Reg would say, "Excuse me, Mr Bruce – he used to call him this even when he was Sir, because he'd got so used to it and not only that, he preferred it – "don't you think you might put that one up in the centre and that one down?" Sir Bruce would go back and he'd put his hands on his hips and say, "That's right, Reg. Just exactly like that." So Reg would have

Mr Bray among the archives of Illustrated Newspapers. *Mid-Thirties.*

to alter the numbers on the backs of the prints, right the way across, like they used to do, left to right, left to right.

'He did this practically to the end. He used to have every paper in the editorial department and he'd take them to the station, or driven with him wherever he was going, back to Penn. He'd always have one set of papers with him, and next morning in the office he'd bring in the page from, say, the *Telegraph* and he'd mark some of the pictures and he'd say, "We must get some pictures on that subject." It was a subject which he thought, "Ah. Make a lovely page."'

That was the single-minded man, a newspaper man in every sense of the term. It was as well that he died before the Thomson takeover. 'The family,' says Bert Bray, 'never for-

October 1975. Mr Bray with the files of the Illustrated London News.

gave Thomson, they never did. And they shed no tears when he died.'

Newspaper and magazine publication has never been a gentle business. The scramble for circulation has been a feature of the trade for more than 250 years and it was at its most naked and brutal in the 1930s, when money was short and bankruptcy always just around the corner. Mr E. W. Willcocks had tough experience of this in the Thirties when he was employed as a newspaper canvasser.

In 1933 most daily papers, together with *The People* and the *News of the World*, took part in schemes to persuade householders and business concerns to change their paper. 'All kinds of gifts were offered to encourage them to do this', Mr Willcocks remembers, 'books, pen and pencil sets, even free insurance against accidents, loss of eyes or limbs, up to £1,000.'

'I worked for Odhams Press in Long Acre. I had no fixed abode. We were based in towns in Kent, Essex, Suffolk, Norfolk and Cambridgeshire for periods of up to three weeks to canvass the town and the district. We worked in teams of ten, with a supervisor and an assistant from the *Daily Herald*.

'It was pretty grim at times. We worked six days a week and had to get a minimum of 55 changes a week. We were paid £3 a week or £3.50 if we were married. Anything over 55 changes earned us an extra 3d. a change. Council estates were good places to work on, because most of the people there voted Labour and the *Herald* was a Labour paper, but, if you got an area of large houses where *The Times* and the *Daily Telegraph* were read, it was hard going.

'The weather was a bugbear, especially if we were working a country district. We were expected to cycle 6 to 10 miles to outlying villages and still get our quota. My wife and I lived in pubs, boarding houses and furnished rooms and, after we'd paid for our board and our travelling expenses, there was nothing left over for luxuries. But we had good and bad times and if you were having a bad day, the other members of the team would help you out. It was a matter of survival in those days of the Depression.

'Newspaper canvassing taught me a lot about human nature.'

Chapter Nine   *What it all adds up to*

The eight chapters in this book represent no more than the sampling of an enormous field. These are an indication of method, an illustration of what is to be done. They are concerned entirely with work and workers in the Midlands, the South and South-West and the London area. Other parts of Britain are equally ripe for attention and would undoubtedly yield just as rich a harvest.

The occupations selected for study cover a wide range and although there was no intention of pursuing themes or special lines of enquiry, certain broad conclusions are possible.

The first – and this was particularly apparent when one met one's informants face to face and spent hours talking to them – is that many, probably a great many, of the people who began work in the Twenties and Thirties, when educational opportunities were theoretically much better than they had been fifty or a hundred years earlier, were obviously employed in jobs far below their intelligence and ability. Had they been born a generation later, or into more fortunately placed families, a proportion of them at least would have received a much longer education and considerably more and more systematic training. These were people who had to earn a living during a period of huge and demoralising unemployment. Their fathers were very likely to be unemployed and they took what work they could find.

Wages and salaries were low, discipline rigid and often autocratic, and working conditions often abominable. It was prudent not to object too strongly or obviously to such things, since the labour market was well stocked and an employer never had any difficulty in filling vacancies. The threat or implied threat of dismissal was usually quite sufficient to bring recalcitrant or rebellious workers to heel and the extent to which people were exploited in such circumstances is almost unbelievable to anyone reared in a gentler and more protective age.

But, as the interviews make clear, there were both good and bad employers, just as there had been in the time of Dickens. The good employers may not always appear particularly enlightened by modern standards, but they have to be measured by the yardstick of their age, and there is no doubt that the people who worked for them realised how fortunate they were. The inter-war years were a period in which anyone with a job did his or her utmost to hold on to it. There was nothing like as much movement from firm to firm as there was between 1945 and 1975, when anyone looking for a change of work was in a sellers' market.

Because so many people reckoned to stay year after year with the same employer, there was, as the interviews reveal so clearly, much more loyalty to the firm than one finds nowadays, a much greater inclination to identify oneself with the place where one worked. Sometimes, it is true, an outside observer begins to doubt if a particular employer really deserved as much loyalty and devotion as he was evidently receiving, but it is difficult to believe that such a situation caused any great harm.

As one passes from interview to interview and from industrial veteran to industrial veteran, one is constantly struck by the sheer size and strength of these people. They were reared in an age in which stoicism, the ability to put up with things and survive, was regarded, and rightly, as the greatest of all virtues. One was unemployed, underpaid, grossly overworked, ill, injured, badly housed, under-educated, tyrannised over, but one made the best of it. The cheerfulness and lack of bitterness among the men and women represented in this book is very remarkable. They accepted, and continue to accept, the human predicament in a way that their children and grandchildren, cosseted by years of wider employment and the Welfare State, have found it impossible to do.

It would not be an exaggeration to say that they worked in an age in which it was considered normal to work hard and to do one's work as well as possible. It may well be that newspapers were produced without printing errors, cafés and restaurants were thoroughly cleaned, and letters were sorted and delivered quickly because public opinion in the Twenties and Thirties saw nothing wrong in getting rid of careless, inefficient workers and replacing them by attentive, responsible workers, but that is not the whole story. These waitresses, glove-cutters, aircraft inspectors, postal sorters and the rest did their job and earned their money in an atmosphere conditioned partly by fear but also by pride. And pride, not only in doing one's job well but in being allowed to do it well, is surely a basic human need and pleasure. The book begins very deliberately with the heart-warming story of the building of Clifton Cathedral, where John Laing gave its employees the very rare opportunity of doing a job perfectly. The way in which they welcomed this makes the case something of a classic in industrial relations and industrial psychology. Clifton Cathedral was a significantly unmodern event.

One cannot, of course, put the clock back, and it is foolish to want to or to try. But there are, even so, certain human needs which are so constant as almost to amount to an instinct. The list is not, perhaps, a very long one, but it assuredly includes doing something really well at least once in one's life and, equally certainly, being valued and respected for what one is and what one does. Over and over again these two human rights are touched on in the interviews, sometimes in a very moving way. There is what amounts almost to an industrial parable, which could be summarised in something like these terms. 'The boss came to me one day and said, "Bill, I can't get this right. I can't see how to do it/improve it/make it work/sell it. Have you got any ideas?" And I said, "Well, I reckon you ought to try this." And he said, "Bill, you're a genius. I simply don't know how we'd get along without you. That's the answer. I should never have thought of it myself."'

This might perhaps be called the indispensability syndrome. It contains, of course, an element of fantasy and occasionally, perhaps, it is pure fantasy, but it expresses the ever-present need to be useful, to be wanted, to have one's worth acknowledged, and it is very unlikely to find fulfilment in a society where people never reckon to stay long in one job. In the strict sense of the word nobody is indispensable, but it is satisfying and encouraging to feel that one may be.

These general thoughts about the past are illustrated in different ways by the men and women who have dug into their memories to help us. The John Laing employees who built Clifton Cathedral explained exactly why it was 'the happiest job I was ever associated with', and described in great detail how the work was carried out, what the snags were and the problems and how they were overcome. They gave us the kind of information we yearn in vain to have from the medieval cathedral builders. The furniture-makers told us about cut-throat competition in the Twenties and Thirties, about good and shoddy work, about keeping going under appallingly difficult war-time conditions, and about the kind of people who bought well-made furniture and the people, much more numerous, who never bought any new furniture at all.

Those with pre-war experience of the catering industry have given us their accounts of working very long hours for very little money, of needing a matriculation certificate to be employed in a dairy in Bournemouth, of pay being stopped for mistakes on the bill or for customers stealing rolls from the next table, of the superior hygienic standards of pre-war days. The glovers have watched the decline and revival of the leather glove, the disappearance of great names in the trade, and the introduction of Japanese machines that knit a complete glove-lining in two minutes. The aeroplane makers experienced the movement from the hard times of the Twenties and Thirties to the boom years of the Second World War, the recruitment of long unemployed skilled men from the old industrial areas, and the autocratic habits of Lord Beaverbrook.

A lady who made biscuits at Peek Freans in Bermondsey talked about the strict discipline there and old-timers at Fortts of Bath revealed the secrets of making the famous Bath Olivers in the traditional way and gave the reasons for the firm's decline and eventual take-over. Two postmen who joined as boy messengers looked back on the service provided in the grand days when Post Offices were open from eight in the morning till eight at night. Men who spent their lives working for newspapers and magazines in one capacity and another tried to put into words what it felt like to be in the business when management was tough, unemployment an ever-present threat, everybody knew everybody else and you just learnt as you went, the hard way.

The message running through all these memories is a simple one. 'It was a matter of survival in those days. We helped one another and we came through somehow.' The same paradox strikes one over and over again – the period of unfettered hire and fire and private enterprise and poor working conditions produced an atmosphere of brotherhood and mutual help among the workers, while the period of socialism, the Welfare State and greatly improved wages and amenities which followed gave rise to a spirit of pushing and shoving, selfishness and I'm-alright-Jack, which most retired workers, with memories of the hard pre-war days find strange and somewhat shocking.

The reconstruction of the spirit of the past, which is what the historian's task is all about, is a tantalisingly difficult business, tantalising because one can never be even reasonably sure that one has got it right or followed the most reliable clues. At the very least, however, it must help to be able to talk with people who have experienced the past, people who were actually there. One may misinterpret what they say, one may ask them the wrong questions, but to have heard their view of events must allow one to work towards a fairer and more complete understanding of what actually happened. History, after all, is the record of a continuous interaction between facts and theories, between people and happenings, between action and ideas. To concentrate on only one or two of these aspects of the past is to make distorted vision a certainty.

Words by themselves, whether spoken or written, are not an adequate vehicle with which to explore and assess the past. Without something one can see and touch, one makes serious and disastrous mistakes and, even with the help of these two senses, something will be missing if one has no opportunity to taste and smell the past. One must, even so, recognise technical and scientific limitations. One day, no doubt, we shall be able to record and preserve tastes and smells for the benefit of posterity, but that is still in the future and these aspects of history must still be allowed to vanish. It would be wonderful to taste a pre-war Bath Oliver biscuit, if only to test the statement made by one of our informants that these famous delicacies, as sold nowadays, bear little resemblance to the real thing that was made half a century ago.

With buildings, photographs and museum objects one can do a good deal better, however. All these kinds of physical evidence of the past are both important and interesting in themselves and acquire added meaning when one is able to relate them to what people with long memories have been able to say about them. To listen to an elderly man or woman talking about his or her work many years ago and then to look at a photograph showing the place referred to helps to bring both the conversation and the picture alive. A catalogue of the firm's products, a price list, a press cutting, or a group of people employed together at the factory has the same effect. The pictures give the reminiscences a framework of proper scale and indicate the passage of time. What especially impresses one so often is the relatively small size of yesterday's operations and the cramped, simple conditions under which they were carried out. A visit to the archaeology, that is, the surviving buildings, makes the point even more clearly. It is not only that industry and commerce today are bigger in every way than they were fifty years ago, they also take place in more anonymous, less human-size surroundings and this must influence the attitudes of the people who work there.

The title of this book, *Where We Used to Work*, consequently means much more than a mere building or part of a building. If one makes what appears on the surface to be a simple request, 'Tell me about the place where you used to work', the result is likely to be far from simple. One will hear about a building or buildings, of course, but one will also have poured into one's ears and tape-recorder all the kinds of information which form the material of this book, facts and opinions about management, wages, discipline, health, colleagues, holidays, everything that adds up to work. None of these things stands on its own, at least in the minds and memories of those directly affected. Taken together they amount to a rough and ready definition of the word 'where', a closely-knit, living complex of people, institutions, equipment and an elusive something for which it is difficult to find a better word than 'atmosphere'. 'Where' is, in fact, chiefly a matter of atmosphere and all the other items to which we have referred are little more than the constituent elements which, working in unison, create the atmosphere of a person's work. It is largely this fact which makes 'working archaeology' so much more satisfactory an expression than 'industrial archaeology'.

Index